IMAGE & ECHO

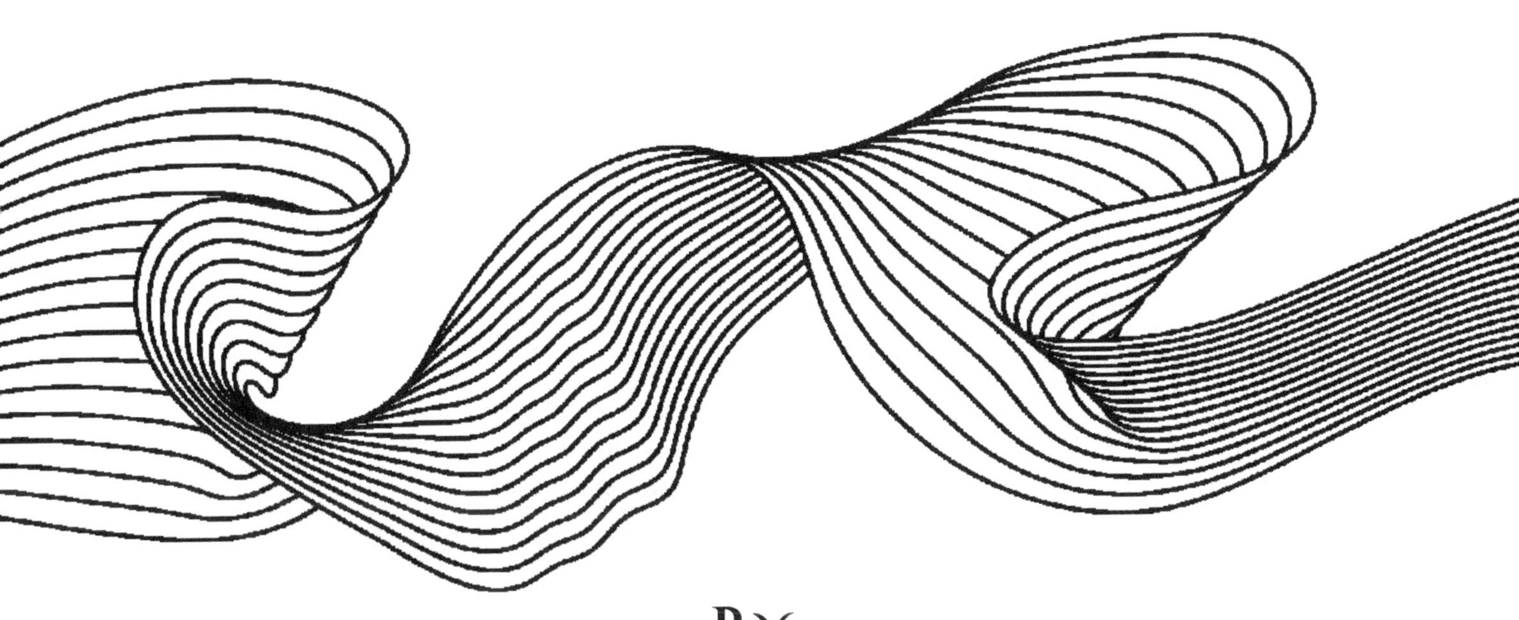

BY

KIERAN BEVILLE

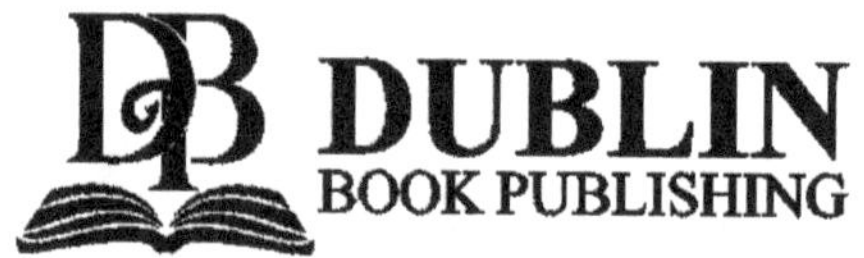

Block 4 Harcourt Rd,
Saint Kevin's, Dublin,
D02 HW77, Ireland

ISBN (Paperback)
ISBN (Hardback)

Cover Design by Dublin Book Publishing

About the Author

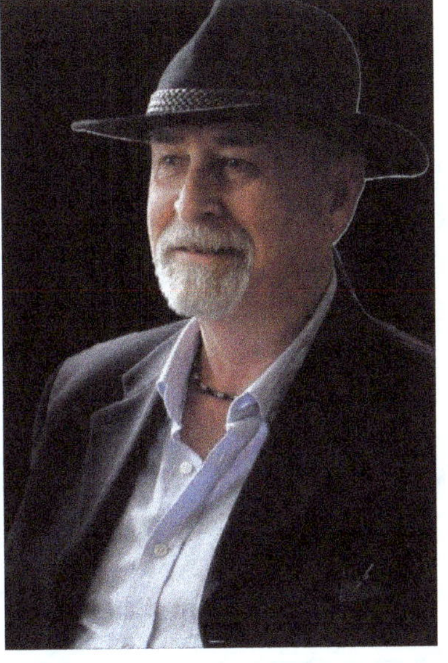

Kieran Beville is a writer/poet with an extensive body of work, having published numerous poems in a wide range of respected journals, magazines and anthologies. In addition to his literary accomplishments, he is also a visual artist who enjoys exploring creativity through painting with oils/acrylics. Beville has authored many articles, often focusing on writers, artists, and musicians, reflecting his deep engagement with the arts. A seasoned scholar and academic, he has published several books across disciplines, including six volumes of poetry, further establishing his reputation as a thoughtful and prolific voice in contemporary literature and culture. He acknowledges that writing *Image & Echo* was a labour of love.

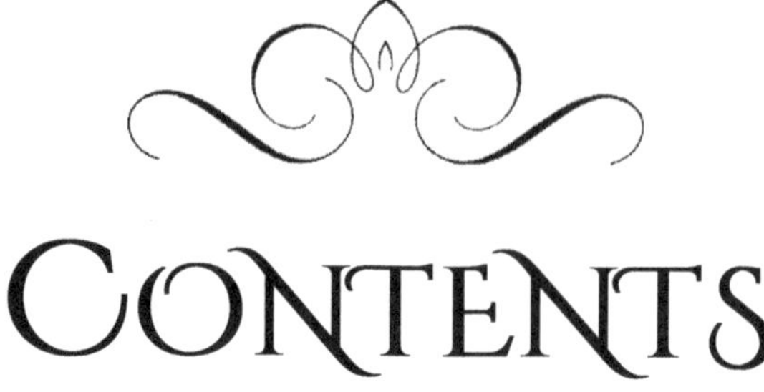

CONTENTS

INTRODUCTION

By way of introduction I should say something about ekphrasis – offer a brief explanation and thereby put this work in context. Ekphrasis is a literary practice where a poem or other work of writing responds to, describes, or reflects upon a visual artwork. More than simple description, ekphrastic poetry seeks to enter into a dialogue with the image—bringing it to life in language, exploring its emotional resonance, and sometimes imagining new stories or perspectives beyond the frame. It is a meeting place between the visual and the verbal, where art inspires art. This book is a gallery of voices: a collection of ekphrastic poems that speak to, with, and sometimes against the images that inspired them.

From the warm stillness of Monet's *Impression, Sunrise* to the wrenching distortion of Picasso's *Weeping Woman*. From the vivid testament of Pain and Power in Frida Kahlo's self-portrait to the intimate quiet of Vermeer's *Girl with a Pearl Earring* to the cosmic turbulence of Van Gogh's *Starry Night*, these poems seek to inhabit the world each painting creates. The result is not description, but transformation—moments where language and image converge.

Many of the works in this volume—such as Botticelli's *Birth of Venus*, Klimt's *The Kiss*, and Caravaggio's *Conversion of Saint Paul*—evoke themes of myth, love, revelation, or loss. Others, like Renoir's *Luncheon of the Boating Party* or Leech's *The Sunshade*, revel in light and leisure. Still others, such as Yeats's *The Liffey Swim* or Rembrandt's *The Night Watch*, offer dynamic glimpses of a moment in motion, a crowd in flux. These poems are acts of close looking, but also of imaginative listening—attending to what the artworks might be saying, or withholding.

Each poem is written in two principal forms – the sonnet and blank verse. The Shakespearean sonnet, built of three quatrains and a couplet (abab cdcd efef gg), offers a structure of development, contrast, and resolution. In contrast, the Petrarchan sonnet, used in response to da Vinci's *Mona Lisa*, divides into an octave and a sestet (abbaabba cdecde), often turning inward, suited to quiet meditation. Blank verse, composed in unrhymed iambic pentameter (10 syllables per line in a repeated pattern – stressed/unstressed) allows for expansive reflection and dramatic tone—it is the voice of soliloquy, the cadence of thought itself.

Some paintings invited broader engagement. Millais's *Ophelia* is accompanied by a triptych of Shakespearean sonnets – one from Hamlet's point of view, one from Gertrude's, and one from a neutral, reflective voice. A blank verse monologue completes the suite, creating a layered portrait of grief and perception.

For Van Gogh's *Starry Night*, the poetic response includes not only a sonnet and blank verse poem, but also a prose poem—an imagined letter from Vincent to his brother Theo—offering a fictional but intimate entry into the artist's mind. Elsewhere, Hockney's *Portrait of an Artist (Pool with Two Figures)*, Gauguin's *Tahitian Women on the Beach*, and Dali's *The Persistence of Memory* prompt lyrical, psychological, and surreal poetic responses.

These poems do not attempt to explain the art. Rather, they accompany it—shadowing the brushstrokes, echoing its light, questioning its silences. In that sense, this is a collection not just of poems about art, but of poems in dialogue with art: a chorus of interpretations, reinterpretations, and imagined afterlives. Read them slowly. Let the image guide the line and the line return you to the image—altered, deepened, made strange or familiar again.

In addition to the poems, this collection includes a brief article for each artwork that tells its story—providing historical context, artistic significance, and the narratives behind the image. These essays are intended to enrich your reading experience and offer deeper insight into the paintings that inspired the poetry.

IMPRESSION SUNRISE – CLAUDE MONET

THE DAWN OF A REVOLUTION IN ART

When Claude Monet stood before the harbour of Le Havre in 1872, he wasn't trying to change the course of art history—he simply wanted to capture the fleeting sensation of dawn breaking over the sea. What he ended up creating, however, was more than just a painting; it was the spark that ignited one of the most radical artistic movements of the modern era.

Titled *Impression, Sunrise* (*Impression, Soleil Levant*), the painting shows a hazy morning scene where smokestacks, rowboats, and the fiery orb of the sun emerge softly from a misty palette of blues and greys. The brushwork is brisk, almost casual, as though Monet were racing against the sun to record what his eyes saw in that exact moment. Unlike the polished realism favoured by the art establishment of the time, this piece embraced atmosphere over accuracy, feeling over form.

When it was exhibited in 1874 as part of a breakaway group of young artists rebelling against the rigid rules of the Paris Salon, a sceptical critic mocked the term "Impression" in the title, claiming the paintings were mere fragments, lacking finish. But what began as an insult quickly became a badge of honour. Monet and his peers adopted the label "Impressionists," proudly aligning themselves with a new vision of art—one that captured movement, mood, and the shifting qualities of light.

Today, *Impression, Sunrise* hangs in the Musée Marmottan Monet in Paris, not just as a beautiful painting, but as the manifesto of a movement. With one canvas and a bold title, Monet helped usher in a new age, where how something is seen mattered just as much as what was seen.

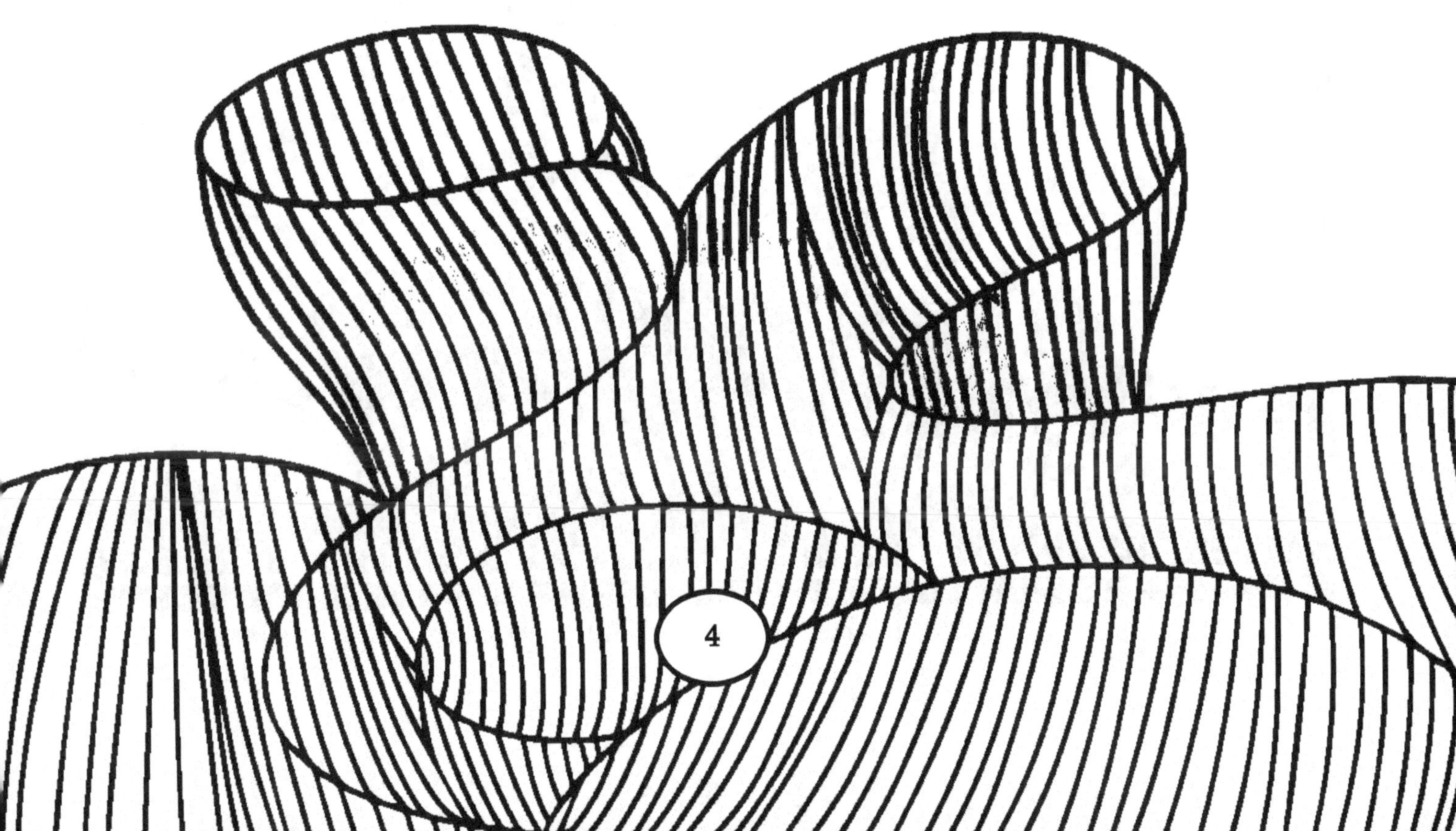

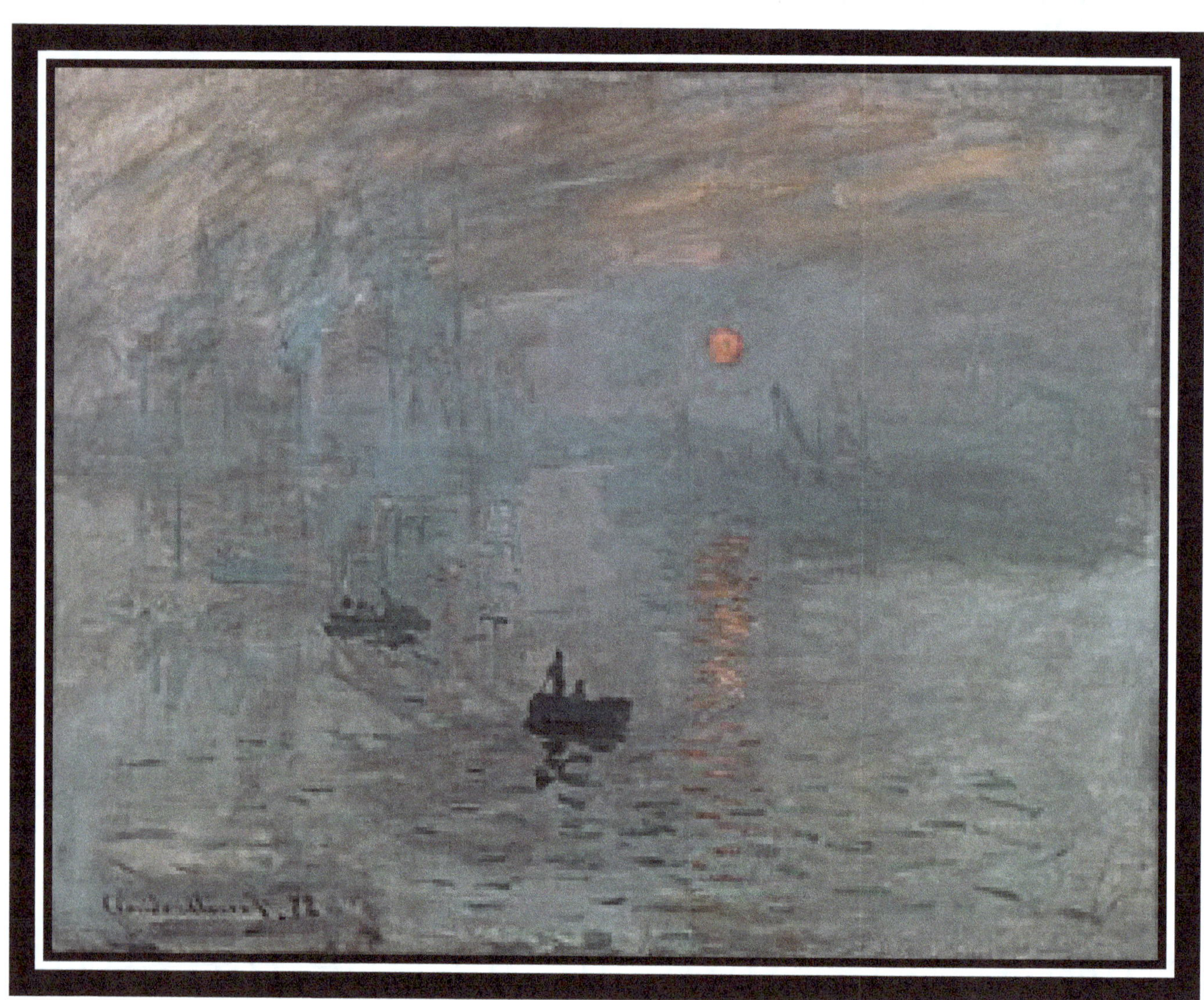

Impression, Sunrise by Claude Monet

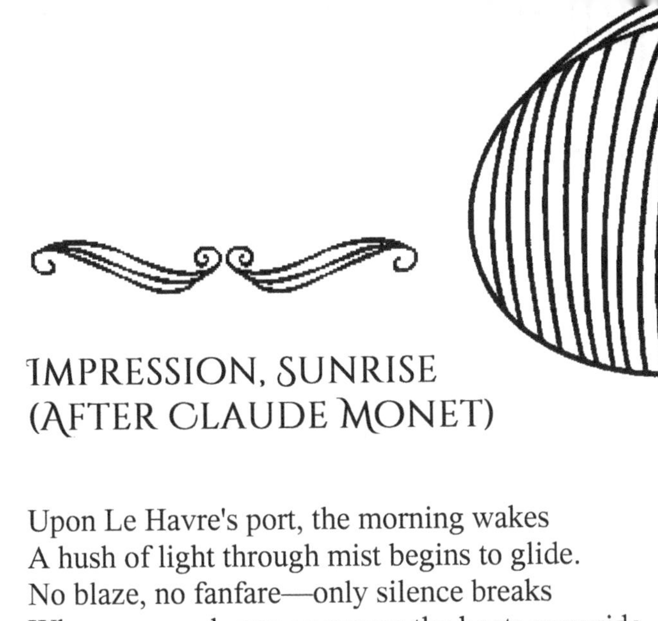

IMPRESSION, SUNRISE
(AFTER CLAUDE MONET)

Upon Le Havre's port, the morning wakes
A hush of light through mist begins to glide.
No blaze, no fanfare—only silence breaks
Where orange burns on waves the boats now ride.

A breath, a blur, a world not sharply drawn
Yet vivid in the stillness it conveys
The harbour stirs beneath a ghostly dawn
Its outlines lost in nature's drifting haze.

Not what we see, but how it strikes the soul—
A fleeting moment held in trembling hue.
The sun, a smudge, yet somehow makes us whole
More real than forms the eye once thought it knew.

So here began a world reframed by light
A truth impression made more clear than sight.

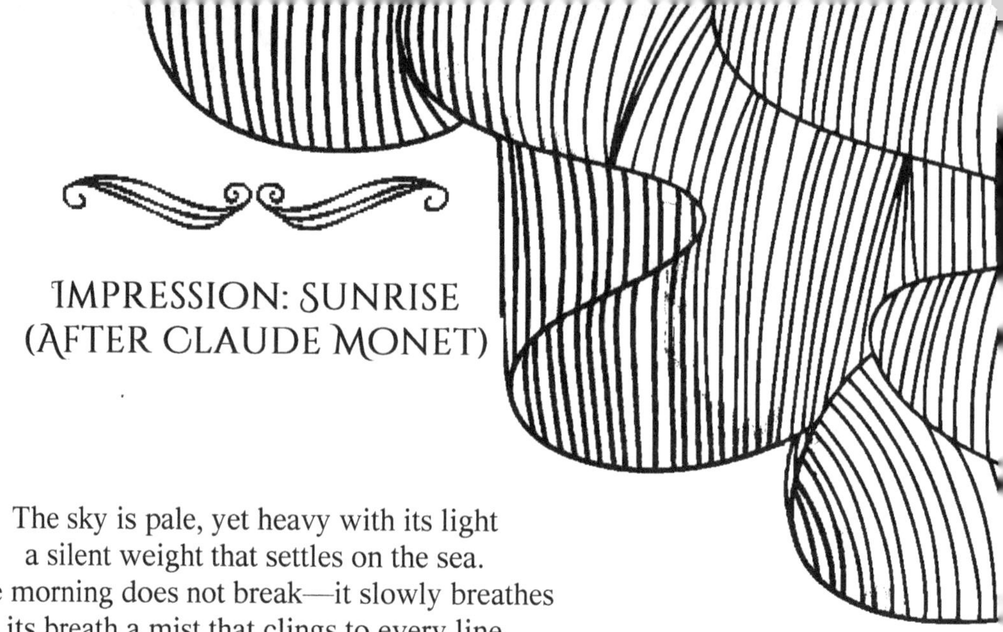

IMPRESSION: SUNRISE
(AFTER CLAUDE MONET)

The sky is pale, yet heavy with its light
a silent weight that settles on the sea.
The morning does not break—it slowly breathes
its breath a mist that clings to every line
and blurs the edge of water, boat, and shore.

The harbour stirs in quiet, muted tones.
No sudden call, no colour cries aloud
a whispered orange trembles near the sun
a flame that does not burn but barely is—
a presence, not a signal or a rule.
The ships are shadows rising from the tide
their masts like reeds caught in a ghostly swell.
Men row in silence, faceless in the fog
as if the sea itself had dreamed of them
and now must let them slip into the world.

I stand before this scene not as I am
but as a breath, a witness uncontained
dissolved into the shimmer of the air.

The oil is wet, yet speaks of light and time.
This canvas does not show the dawn—it feels it.
The chill, the drift, the hush between the strokes
where every colour hovers, unresolved.

And this is art – to paint not what is seen
but what it means to see. To catch the trace
of one small hour between the dark and day
and say, "I was alive, and this was morning."
No lines are sharp. The world is born in blur
and still it moves, and still it asks for more.

What do we know of light until it fades?
What do we know of time until it slips
like water through the frame we try to fix?
Yet here it is—the moment and its ghost
a harbour half-awake, the sea unsure
a painter with his easel in the cold
and all of life beginning with a haze.

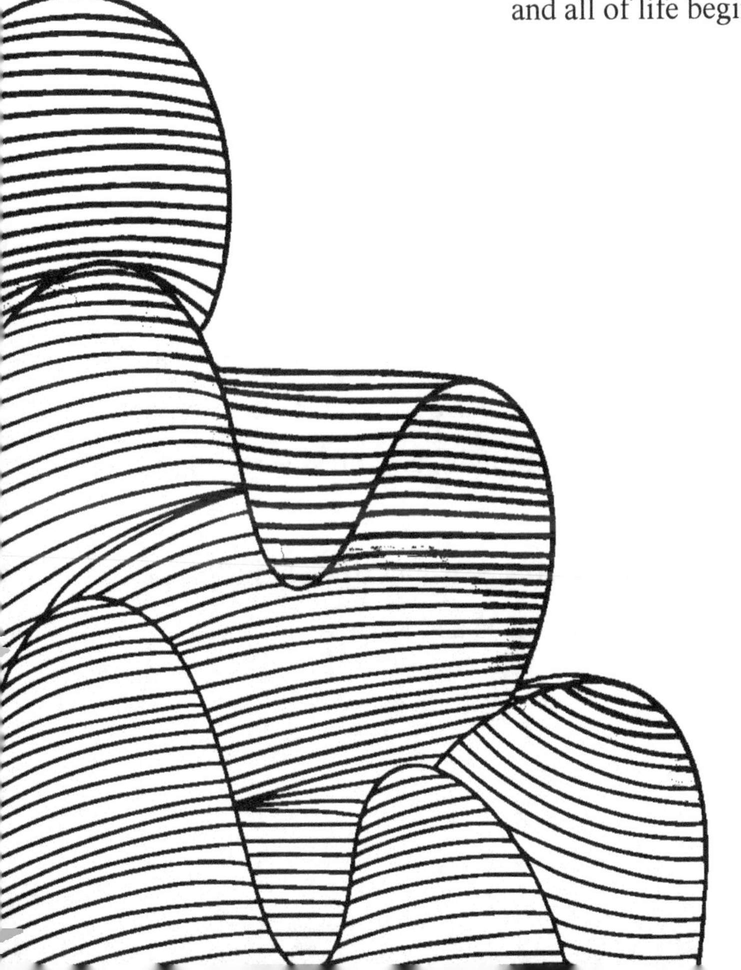

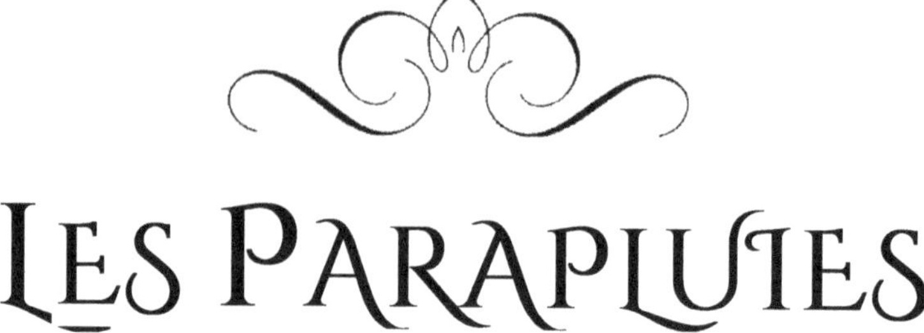

LES PARAPLUIES

RENOIR'S MASTERPIECE OF TRANSITION AND TENSION

Pierre-Auguste Renoir's *Les Parapluies* (*The Umbrellas*) is a painting not merely admired for its elegance, but studied for the way it captures a society in flux—visually, socially, and even artistically. Created in two distinct phases between circa 1881 and 1886, the painting stands as one of the clearest records of a pivotal moment—not just in the lives of its subjects, but in Renoir's own creative evolution.

A TALE OF TWO STYLES

What makes *Les Parapluies* so remarkable is not only what it shows, but how it shows it. Renoir began the painting around 1881 using the Impressionist style he had helped pioneer. You can see this particularly in the left half of the canvas: the women with light, airy dresses rendered in loose brushwork and a bright colour palette.

But Renoir, disenchanted with Impressionism's fleeting effects, had by 1883 turned toward a more structured, classical approach, influenced by his study of Ingres and Renaissance masters.

WHY INGRES MATTERS TO RENOIR AND LES PARAPLUIES?

Around 1881–1883, Renoir became disillusioned with Impressionism. Though he was a central figure in that movement, he began to feel that its emphasis on fleeting light and momentary impressions lacked structure and permanence. He later wrote that he felt like he had "reached the end of Impressionism."

During this transitional period, Renoir travelled to Italy, where he studied Raphael and other Renaissance masters. But it was Jean-Auguste-Dominique Ingres, the 19th-century French Neoclassical painter, who had a particularly strong influence. Ingres was known for his precise line work, clear smooth modelling of figures and a revival of classical composition and anatomical clarity.

Renoir admired Ingres's ability to give form and structure to the human body, something he felt was missing from his own work up to that point. This encounter with Ingres's ideals sparked what is often called Renoir's "Ingres period" (roughly 1883–1887). In *Les Parapluies*, you see both worlds. On the left, painted around 1881, you have classic Impressionist techniques—broken brushstrokes, lighter colours, shimmering detail.

On the right, completed after 1885: You can see Renoir's turn toward Ingres—solid contours, restrained palette, and a more sculptural treatment of the mother and children.

The two styles are visible side by side on the same canvas, making Les Parapluies a kind of living document of Renoir's stylistic evolution.

So yes, when critics and historians say Renoir was "influenced by Ingres" in *Les Parapluies*, they're referring specifically to this mid-career shift toward classical drawing, strong composition, and clearly defined form, inspired by Ingres and other classical painters. This stylistic dichotomy divides the canvas almost in half – one part Impressionist, the other part Classical, a rare phenomenon in a single finished work.

THE SOCIAL SNAPSHOT

Set on a Parisian street, likely Montmartre, *Les Parapluies* depicts a crowd caught in a sudden rain. But this isn't merely a study of weather—it's a subtle reflection on social class and human interaction.

A woman holds an empty basket and a young girl stares outward with striking directness, involving the viewer in the scene. All around, umbrellas cluster and tilt, creating a canopy of blue and grey.

RAIN WITHOUT RAIN – AN ARTISTIC ILLUSION

One of the most curious aspects of *Les Parapluies* is what's missing – actual rain. There are no raindrops, no puddles and no dark clouds. Instead, the umbrellas themselves tell the story. This absence allows the focus to remain on human gesture and gaze—on the tension of the moment rather than the weather itself.

RENOIR IN TRANSITION

Les Parapluies is not just a snapshot of Parisian life—it's a snapshot of Renoir's artistic transition. Around this time, he declared Impressionism "a blind alley" and began searching for permanence over atmosphere. This painting, with its mix of free Impressionist spontaneity and solid Neoclassical construction, is his bridge between two worlds.

Notably, the painting was left unsigned and was still in Renoir's studio at the time of his death, suggesting he may have viewed it as a personal exploration rather than a showpiece.

LEGACY

Now housed in the National Gallery in London (on long-term loan from the Hugh Lane Gallery in Dublin), *Les Parapluies* remains one of the most studied and beloved works in Renoir's oeuvre—not just for its beauty, but for its rare honesty about change. It doesn't capture a single moment—it captures a moment undergoing change – in weather, in social roles, and in the very hand of the artist who painted it.

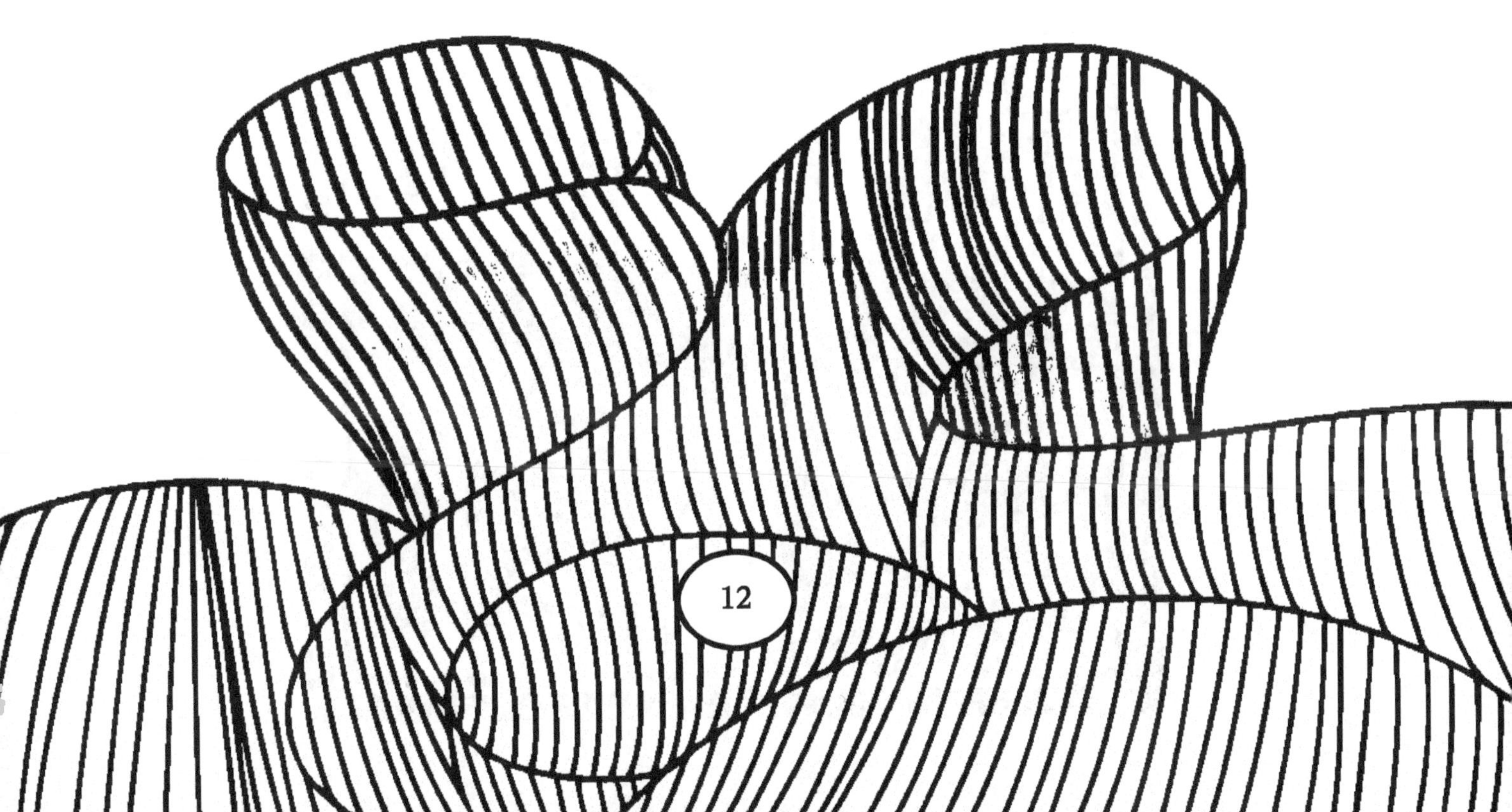

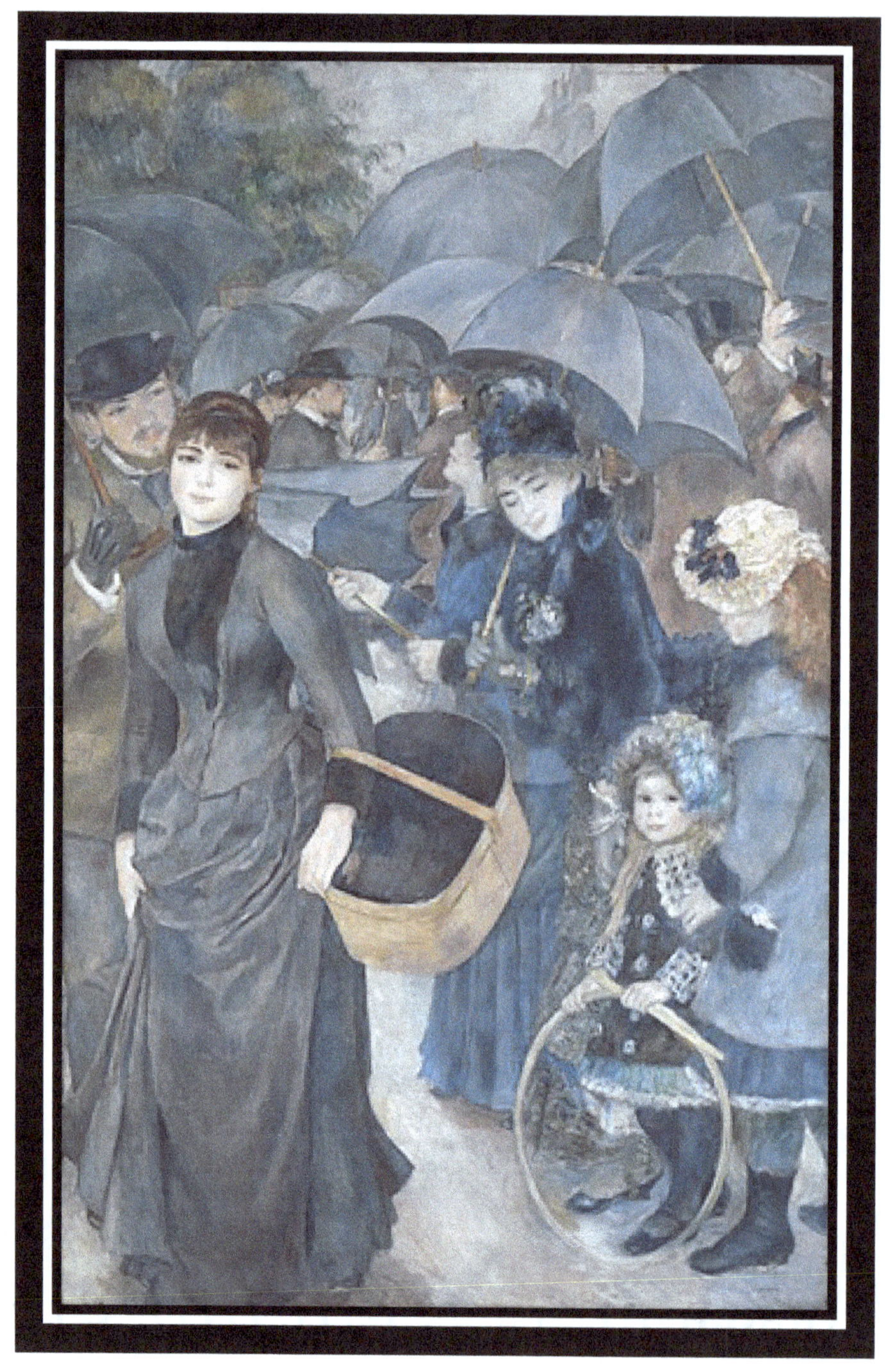

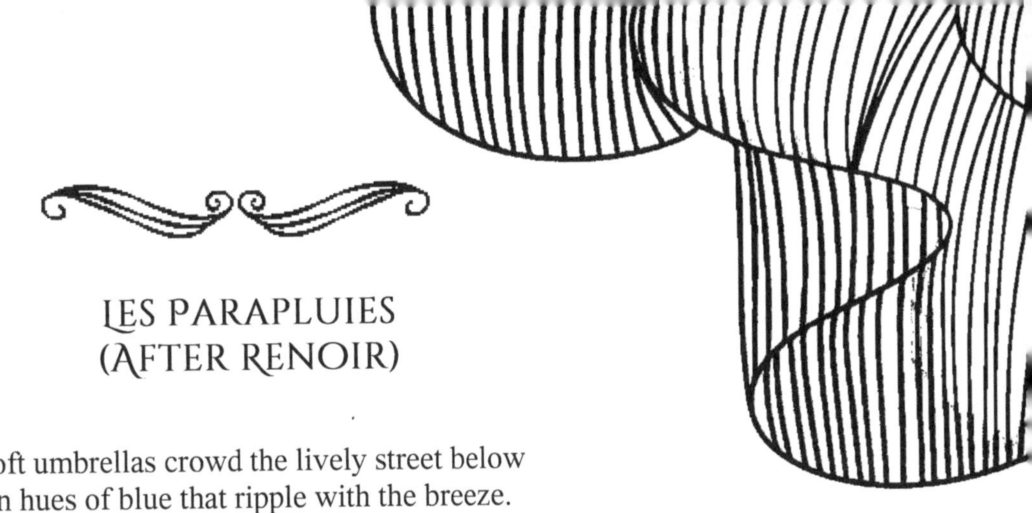

LES PARAPLUIES
(AFTER RENOIR)

Soft umbrellas crowd the lively street below
in hues of blue that ripple with the breeze.
Two girls in bonnets, moving calm and slow
the younger's eyes meet ours with quiet ease.

A woman walks alone, her head unshorn
her dress flows loose around her ankle's sweep.
An empty basket, by her side, is borne—
a silent story she alone can keep.

Behind, a man leans in with open shade
his umbrella arcs in gentle appeal.
She turns away, her answer left unsaid
her face a secret none can coax or steal.

Between the shelter and the open air
we find ourselves suspended, unaware.

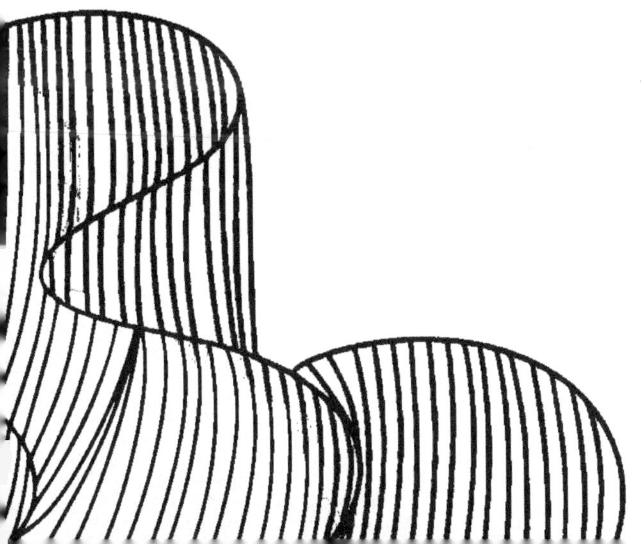

LES PARAPLUIES
(AFTER RENOIR)

A crowd moves forward, umbrellas rise—
soft blues and greys like petals in the air.
Above them, only tree tops shimmer faint
a leafy fringe against a cloudy sky,
no trunks to hold them firm, just whispers there.

Two girls walk close, both bonneted and calm—
the younger holds a hula hoop and looks
directly out, her gaze both steady, bright.

At centre, a woman walks bareheaded
her dress sways loose to brush her ankles.
An empty basket hangs along her arm—
a quiet absence in the bustling street.
Behind her, a man leans in with umbrella
offering shelter, soft and hesitating.
She turns her face away, half veiled, apart
part of the flow, yet set distinctly free.

The painter catches movement in the pause—
not frozen still, but breathing, caught between
the lift of dress, the glance that turns away
the pulse that lingers where the light meets rain.

We live within such moments, caught and brief
between the shelter given and declined

uncertain what we hold, what slips away
what fills our hands, and what we leave behind.

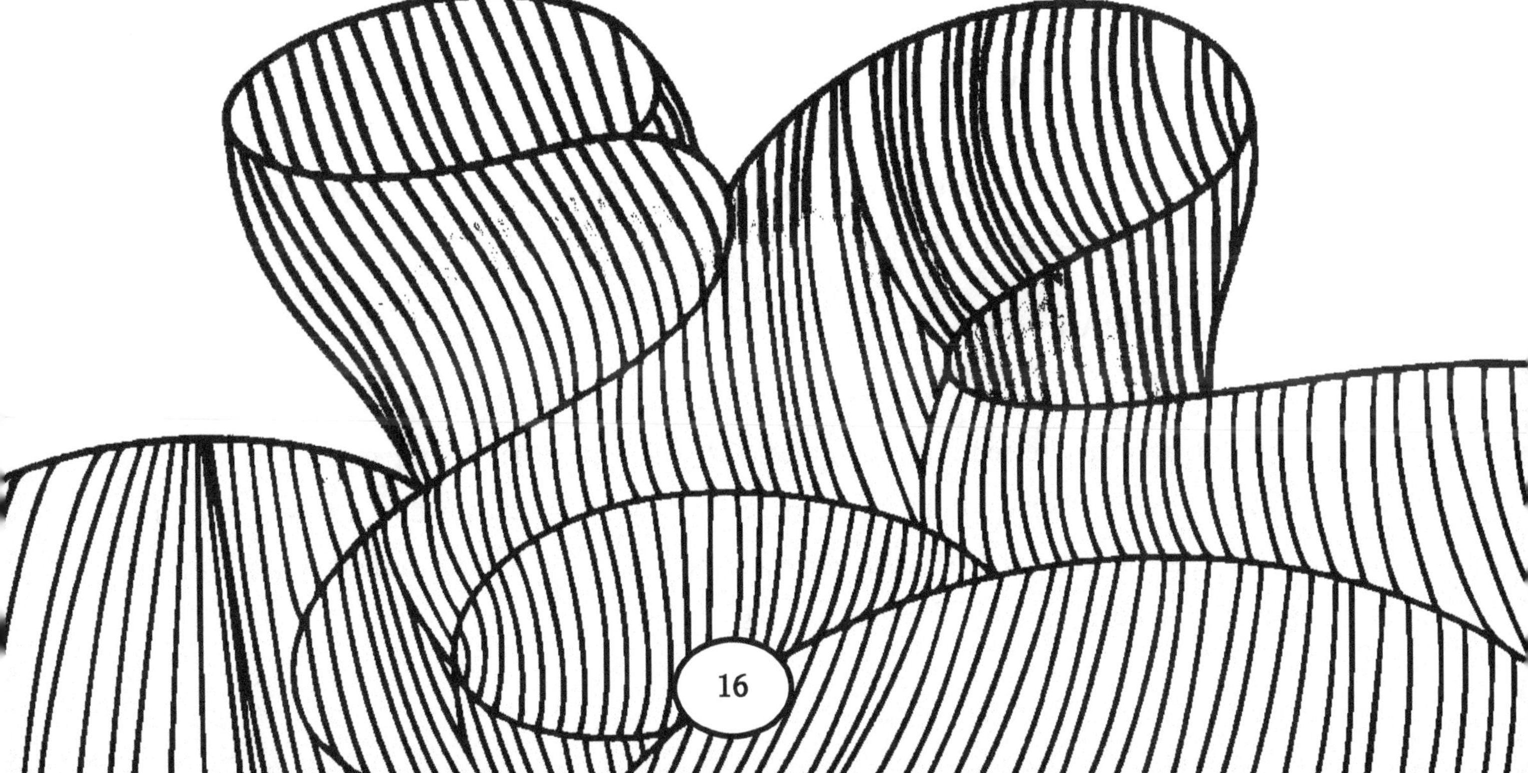

WHISPERS IN WATERCOLOUR

THE TIMELESS ACHE OF MEETING ON THE TURRET STAIRS

In the quiet hush of the National Gallery of Ireland, a singular image continues to pull viewers into a world where love is both a flame and a farewell. Frederic William Burton's *Meeting on the Turret Stairs* (1864) is not a large painting, nor is it rendered in flamboyant colour or bold oil strokes. And yet, its intensity is undeniable. Painted in watercolour and gouache on paper—a medium typically associated with lightness—Burton defies expectation and creates a work that pulses with solemn, aching passion.

A SILENT DRAMA

The painting captures a fleeting moment: a knight and a maiden caught in a wordless goodbye. The woman, dressed in flowing medieval garb, whose back is turned as he descends a stone stairway. Her arms encircle his shoulders gently, almost reverently, while he tilts his helmeted head toward her, eyes closed. No kiss is exchanged; no overt gesture of romantic abandon. And yet, in this arrested motion, an entire narrative unfolds.

Burton was inspired by a Danish ballad—*Agnes and the Elf Knight*—which tells the story of forbidden love. The artist distilled the entire tale into this one crystalline instant, choosing not to tell a story in sequence, but to evoke an emotion that stretches far beyond its single frame. What we witness is not the romance's height, but its end—the last embrace, the unspoken goodbye, the unbearable restraint of love denied.

THE POWER OF WHAT'S NOT SAID

There's a curious power in Burton's decision to avoid overt dramatization. Rather than overt tears or dramatic poses, he opts for subtle gestures—a hand that lingers, a cheek that does not quite touch. The figures are elongated, their postures stylised, evoking a Pre-Raphaelite sensibility. Not unlike the richly detailed works of Rossetti or Millais, Burton's image is ghostlike, suspended in time and bathed in silence. The watercolour medium helps this effect, giving the work a diaphanous, almost dreamlike quality.

Moreover, Burton made a bold artistic choice: the painting was never meant to be displayed permanently. It was designed as a private meditation, a poetic image meant to be viewed occasionally and with reverence. This adds to its mystique—it's a painting that guards its emotions, asking the viewer to lean in closer, as if overhearing a secret.

A PAINTER'S RESTRAINT, A LOVER'S PASSION

Frederic William Burton was not a prolific painter, and his fame today rests largely on this one image. He was also a curator and scholar—eventually serving as the Director of the National Gallery in London. His academic background shows in his meticulous detail and historical reverence. But in *Meeting on the Turret Stairs*, he moves beyond antiquarian interest. This is not a dry re-enactment of medieval life, but a human moment so tender and private that it transcends era and costume.

That tension between distance and intimacy defines the painting. The turret stair itself becomes more than architecture; it's a symbol of their separation, the descending spiral that leads him away from her forever. In many ways, this is not just a depiction of doomed love, but of the haunting moment love becomes memory.

LEGACY AND DEVOTION

In a world saturated with loud declarations of love, *Meeting on the Turret Stairs* remains powerful because of its stillness. It suggests that love's most profound expressions often occur not in action, but in restraint. That fleeting seconds—a hand on armour, a final glance—can contain volumes.

Today, the painting is a national treasure in Ireland, often voted among the country's favourite artworks. Its lasting popularity may lie in the fact that almost everyone has known a version of this moment: the goodbye we never wanted to say, the embrace that could not last. Burton painted not just a medieval tale, but an eternal one.

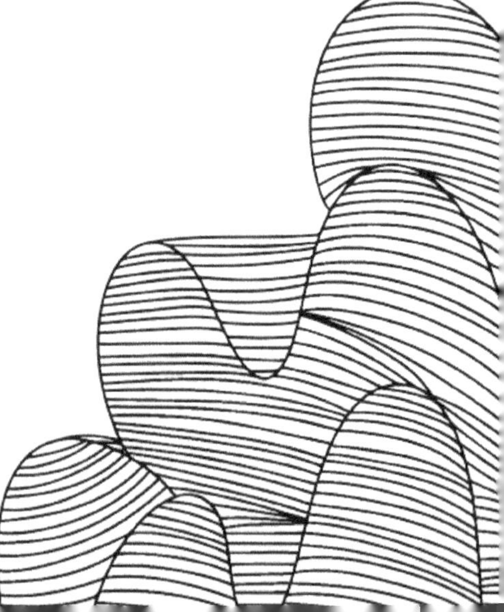

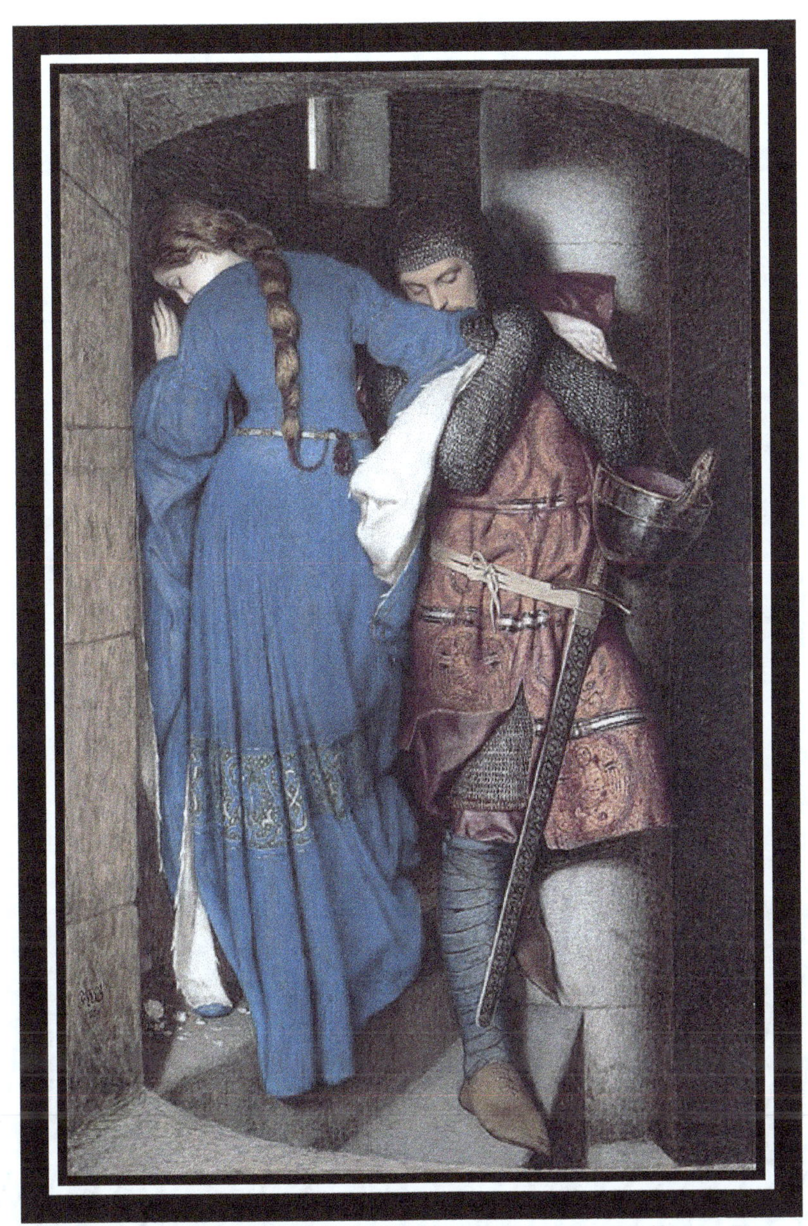

Meeting on the Turret Stairs by Frederic William Burton

HELLELIL AND HILDEBRAND ON THE TURRET STAIRS
(AFTER FREDERIC WILLIAM BURTON)

Upon the stair where twilight softly weaves
Two souls converge in silence, fierce and true
Though bound by walls that fate or kin conceives
Their eyes confess what lips must not pursue.

She leans toward him, breathless, pale with grace
While he, in armour, trembles at her near
No war could strike so deeply as her face
No sword more sharp than love held back by fear.

Yet in that glance, the world dissolves to flame—
A touch, a breath, and time itself is stilled.
No law can cage the heart that dares to name
A love so vast, so tender, and so willed.

Though parted soon, their souls remain aware
One timeless kiss, forever on the stair.

THE TURRET STAIR
(AFTER FREDERIC WILLIAM BURTON)

They stand together on the winding stair
but speak no word, and barely breathe at all.
She turns away — not out of shame or fear
but in the stillness of a heart resigned.
Her face is hidden, pale against the stone
her golden hair like fire against the dusk.
She does not move, but lets the moment be.

Her gown is blue — a deep, resplendent hue
that clings to grief, and lineage, and grace.
She is a lady, bound by blood and law
and he, her guard, must never cross that line.
Yet here, between the stone and dying light,
he dares to lift his hand — gloved, armoured, slow —
and touch the skin laid bare above her sleeve.

He does not seize, or tremble, or demand.
His fingers curve along her tender arm
as though to memorise what cannot last
to say, through touch, what lips may never form.
And she — she does not pull away or flinch
but lets his hand remain, as though she knows
this moment is the last they'll ever have.

No vow is sworn. No future waits beyond.
The world outside would tear them both apart.

But in this stairwell steeped in dying light
their bodies meet in reverent, hushed farewell.

A love forbidden, yet more true than oaths—
not for its fire, but for the flame it hides.
They do not speak; the silence says it all:
a farewell sealed in one unspoken touch.
No future waits. No promise can be kept.
And yet, in that brief contact, they are whole.

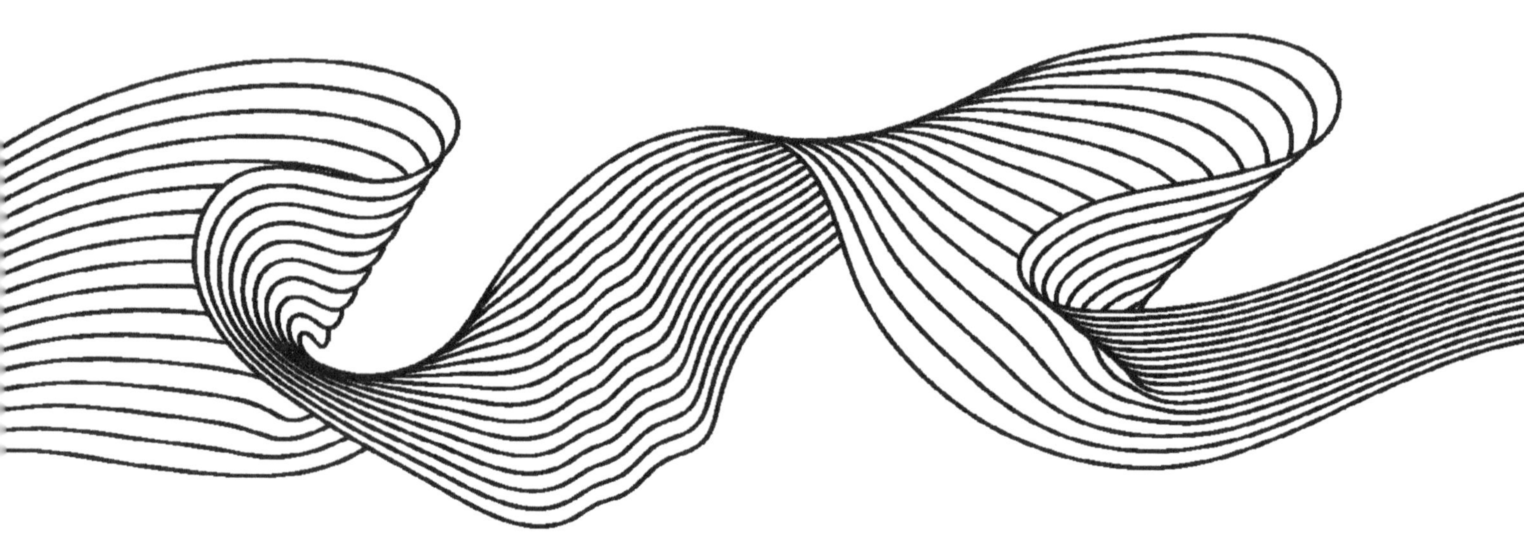

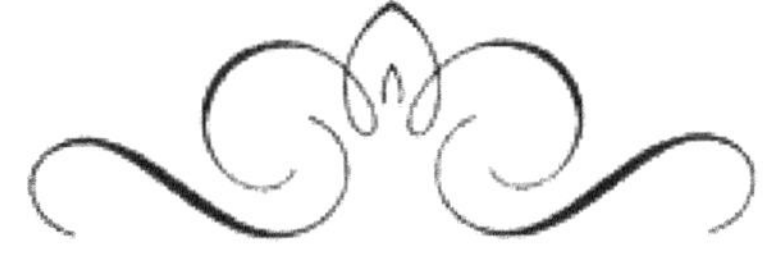

THE PULSE OF A CITY

REDISCOVERING REMBRANDT'S *NIGHT WATCH*

In the dim, thunderous brilliance of Rembrandt van Rijn's *The Night Watch* (1642), something extraordinary happens: a painting breaks loose from the frame of history and strides, almost militarily, into the present. Far from a mere group portrait of Amsterdam's civil militia, *The Night Watch* is a living tableau—chaotic, kinetic, and charged with a psychological depth rarely seen in seventeenth-century Dutch art. It does not just capture a moment; it captures momentum.

A MARCH, NOT A POSE

At first glance, *The Night Watch* appears to follow the conventions of its genre: wealthy militia members immortalized in oil. But Rembrandt defies expectations. The men do not stand in a static formation; they *move*. Captain Frans Banning Cocq, in black with a red sash, and his lieutenant, Willem van Ruytenburch, in golden-yellow, stride forward—not as symbols of calm order, but as participants in a moment thick with purpose. Behind them, a swirl of figures: drummers, arquebusiers[1], a young girl inexplicably bathed in light, and dozens of faces half-caught in motion.

Rembrandt transformed a civic commission into a cinematic drama, compressing action, shadow, and spontaneity into a grand narrative that teems with energy. The canvas, originally over 14 feet wide, seems even larger in imagination. It doesn't just hang on a wall—it occupies space.

THE ALCHEMY OF SHADOW AND LIGHT

Much has been made of Rembrandt's chiaroscuro—his manipulation of darkness and light. But in *The Night Watch*, the contrast is not merely visual; it is emotional and narrative. The darkness is not empty. It hums with anticipation. The light does not merely reveal—it selects. The golden child in the background, her function ambiguous (perhaps a mascot, perhaps allegory), glows with symbolic weight. Her illuminated face and chicken claws—yes, claws—tied to her belt suggest mystery, perhaps even sacrifice.

Rembrandt's lighting is theatrical, but not artificial. It isolates moments the way memory does—imprecisely, but meaningfully. You remember the captain's extended hand, the glint of armour, the smoky background. The gaps are filled by intuition. It's as though the painting recognises that realism is less truthful than impression.

---

[1] During the 15th and 16th centuries, arquebusiers were infantry troops equipped with the arquebus, an early form of long gun.

A SOCIETY IN MICROCOSM

Though a civic militia was meant to symbolise unity and order, *The Night Watch* reveals subtle fractures. The social hierarchy is clear—the wealthy men push to the front while others fade into obscurity. Yet within that hierarchy, individuality seeps through. Each figure bears the trace of a lived life: furrowed brows, careless poses, distracted glances.

In the act of rendering the collective, Rembrandt preserves the personal. This was radical. It speaks of a shifting Dutch society, increasingly affluent, increasingly self-aware, grappling with identity and representation. In a way, *The Night Watch* is not just about these men—it is about the role of the individual in a society learning to define itself.

THE PAINTING AS SURVIVOR

The Night Watch has lived many lives. It was trimmed in the 18th century to fit a new space, losing key elements. It endured attacks—once slashed by a knife, once sprayed with acid. Through all this, the painting has not only survived; it has continued to evolve. It has become a symbol not just of Rembrandt's genius, but of Amsterdam itself—vulnerable, resilient, unfinished.

MORE THAN A MASTERPIECE

To call *The Night Watch* a masterpiece is to understate its strange, enduring vitality. It is not a relic of the past but a provocation to the present. It asks: What do we choose to see? Who stands at the centre, and who is pushed into the margins? What does it mean to remember, and what do we forget?

In Rembrandt's tumult of shadow and movement, we see not just a company of men—we see ourselves: marching, uncertain, luminous, and forever in motion.

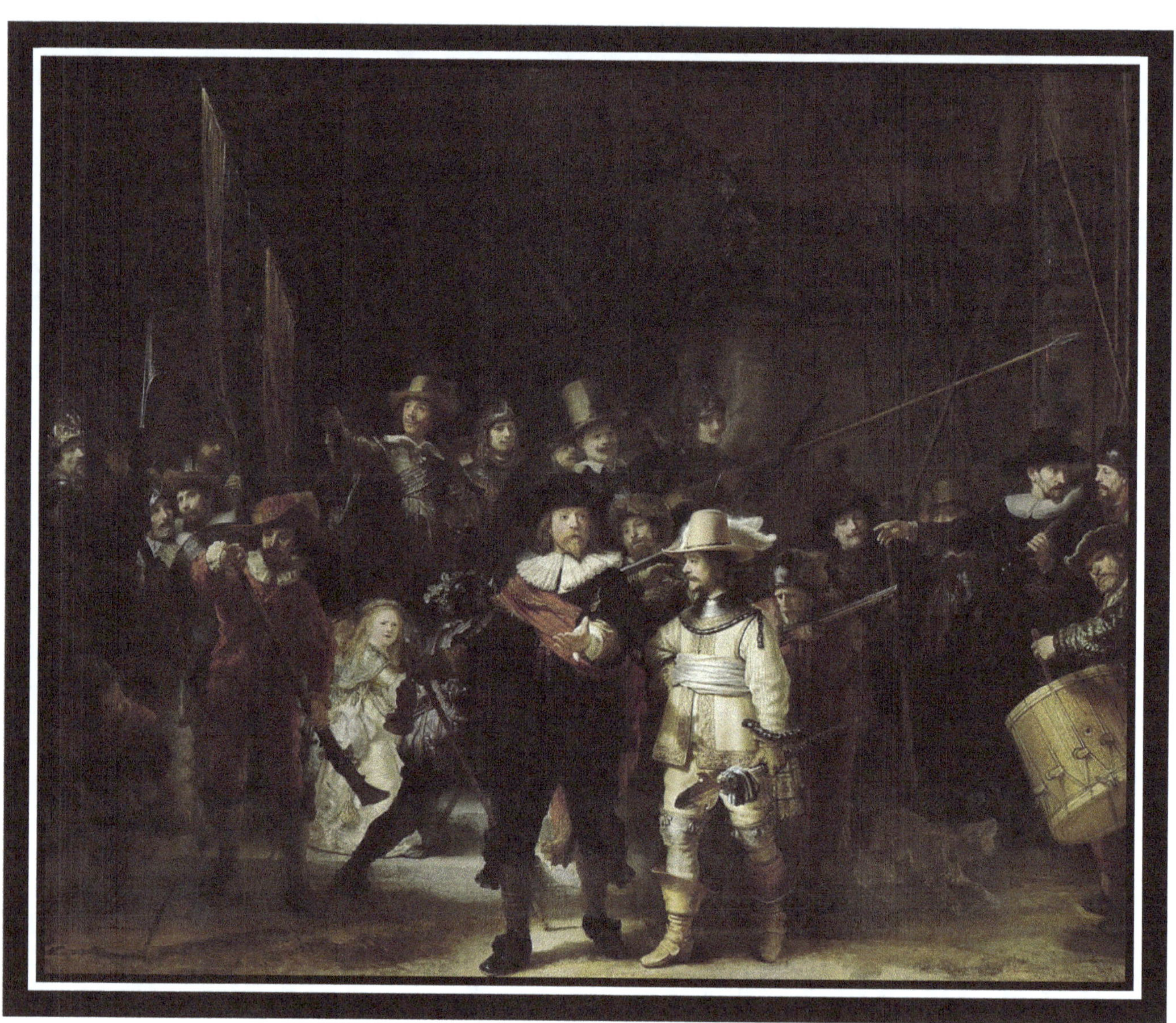

NIGHT WATCH
(AFTER REMBRANDT)

In shadowed streets, the militia takes their stand
A restless crowd alive with light and shade.
Each figure cast by master's careful hand
In chiaroscuro's dance, their roles displayed.

The captain points, a beacon in the dark
While comrades rally, ready for the call.
The girl with chicken, glowing like a spark
Draws focus through the chaos of the hall.

Not still, but caught mid-motion, fierce and proud
The guard prepares to march through dawn's first gleam.
Rembrandt's brush commands the murmuring crowd
Their faces lit by hope and shared esteem.

Through smoky depths, their story boldly told
A timeless watch, in paint and spirit bold.

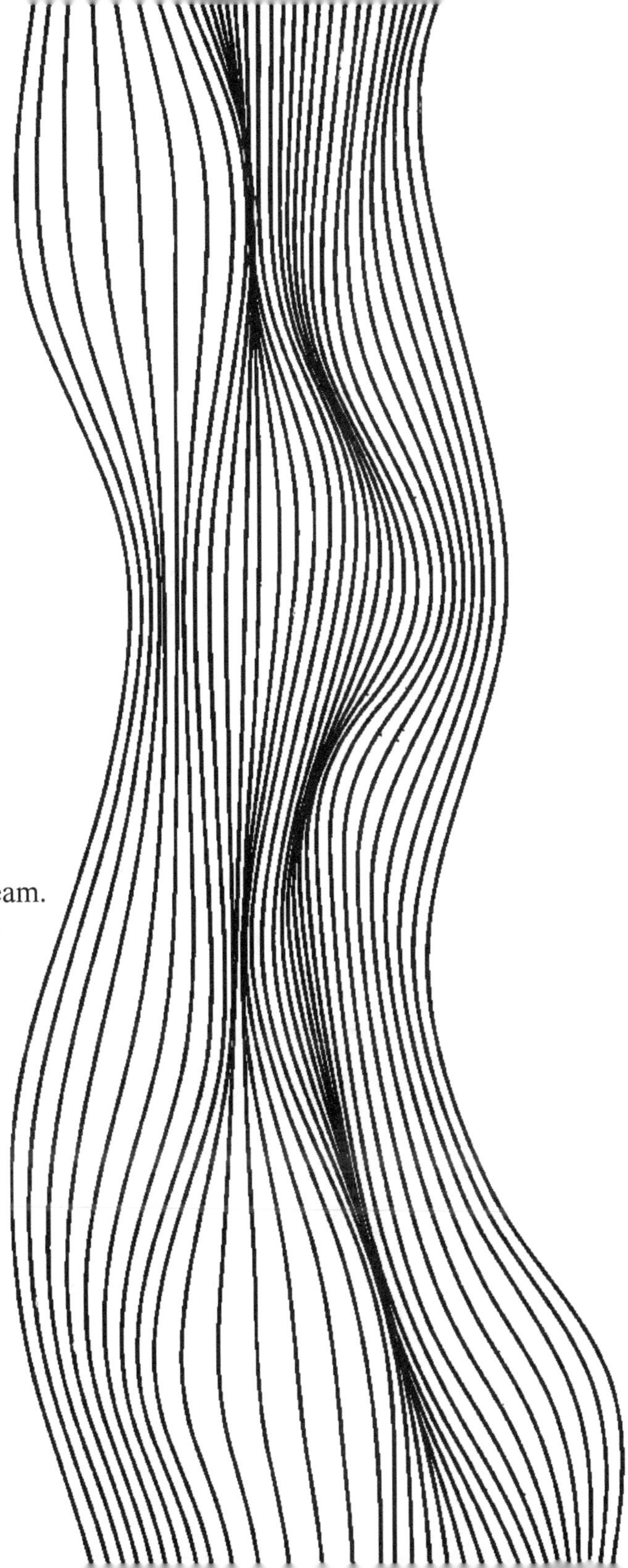

NIGHT WATCH
(AFTER REMBRANDT)

They gather in the dim-lit city square
A band of civic guards prepared for night.
The captain steps ahead with steady gaze
His hand outstretched to lead them into dawn.

Each face is etched with purpose and resolve
Yet caught between the moments, still and swift
A soldier loading muskets, others raise
Their weapons, poised to meet an unknown threat.

The girl with chicken, glowing softly there
A symbol strange amidst the rugged men
Draws eyes like fireflies within the gloom
Her light a quiet pulse in shadow's grip.

The air is thick with tension, breath held tight
As figures blend and part in restless dance
The glow of lanterns catching on the steel
The textures of their coats, worn hats, and boots.

Not idle, but alive with latent power
They stand as one—a force prepared to move.
The painter's brush commands this frozen storm
Where movement meets the stillness of the frame.

Rembrandt's hand reveals the soul beneath
The silent oath to guard and to protect
A moment stretched beyond the bounds of time
Held fast within the canvas' restless heart.

And through the years their watch remains unbroken
A living testament in light and shade—
Not merely soldiers in a city's keep
But guardians of a story etched in gold.

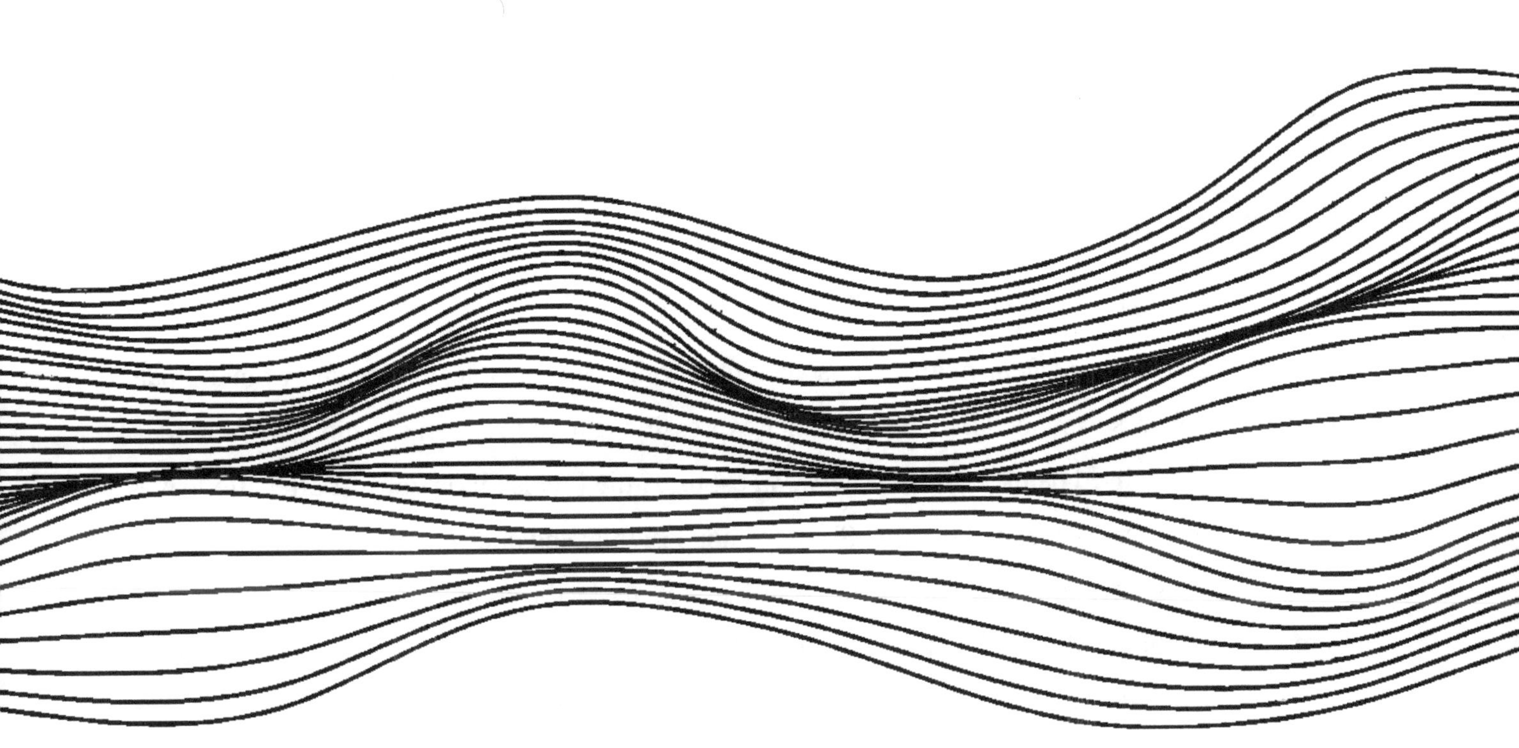

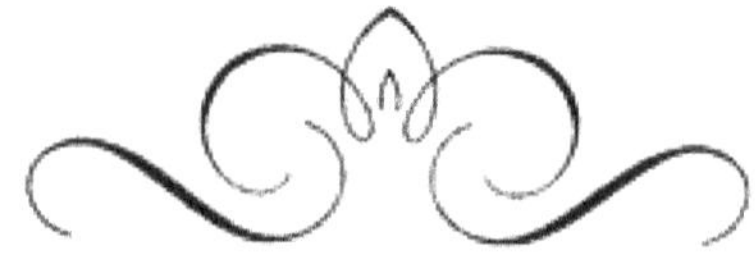

DROWNING IN BEAUTY

A FRESH LOOK AT JOHN EVERETT MILLAIS' OPHELIA

In the lush entanglement of nature and tragedy, few paintings evoke such haunting resonance as John Everett Millais' *Ophelia* (1851–52). Often admired for its technical brilliance and ethereal composition, this seminal work by the Pre-Raphaelite Brotherhood is more than a poetic death scene—it's a revolutionary convergence of realism, symbolism, and Victorian cultural anxieties.

A PORTRAIT OF DEATH, NOT DYING

At first glance, *Ophelia* might be mistaken for a romanticised tableau. A young woman floats serenely in a river, surrounded by wild flora, her expression caught between serenity and surrender. But this is no idealised damsel. Millais' *Ophelia* captures the precise moment just after life leaves the body—a moment suspended in time. She does not struggle; she does not sink. She simply *is*.

This passivity, however, is a deceptive stillness. It masks the complexity of what Millais was attempting to achieve. Rather than focusing on the theatrical demise of Shakespeare's tragic heroine from *Hamlet*, he gives us a scene where nature itself becomes complicit, even indifferent, to human suffering.

NATURE – WITNESS OR CULPRIT?

A hallmark of the Pre-Raphaelite movement was its almost obsessive attention to detail, and Millais was its exemplar. The botanical accuracy in *Ophelia* is not decorative—it is narrative. Each plant has symbolic meaning: the poppies for death, the violets for faithfulness, the daisies for innocence. The nettles and willows are not just background foliage; they tell the story as much as the figure of Ophelia herself.

Millais spent months painting the riverbank of the Hogsmill River in Surrey, braving inclement weather and reportedly contracting illness from prolonged exposure. This commitment wasn't merely for visual effect. It grounded *Ophelia* in a tangible reality. The natural world, meticulously rendered, is not romanticised—it is wild, tangled, and indifferent. It is both stage and silent character, underscoring a Victorian unease with nature's power and inscrutability.

THE MODEL AND THE MYTH

Elizabeth Siddal, the model for Ophelia, adds another layer of melancholy. A muse to several Pre-Raphaelite artists and later wife to Dante Gabriel Rossetti, Siddal herself became an icon of tragic beauty. During the painting sessions, she lay fully clothed in a bathtub of cold water heated by candles—candles that famously went out, leading to a severe cold. Her own life, marked by illness and early death, echoes eerily with the fate of the character she portrayed.

THE FEMININE SUBLIME

Millais' *Ophelia* can also be read through the lens of Victorian attitudes toward femininity and madness. In Shakespeare's play, Ophelia's descent into madness is framed as a response to grief, loss, and patriarchal control. Millais amplifies this by stripping her of agency in the painting—she floats not as a subject but as an object, passive and surrounded. Yet, in her stillness, there is power. She becomes a martyr of emotion, of beauty, of art itself.

This visual quietude resists the melodramatic conventions of the time. Unlike other depictions of Ophelia, Millais' version denies viewers the comfort of spectacle. Her tragedy is not loud—it's suffocating in its calm.

LEGACY IN BLOOM

More than 170 years after its creation, *Ophelia* continues to captivate and unsettle. In an age where beauty and death are often sanitised or sensationalised, Millais' vision lingers as a quiet rebellion. It reclaims the often-overlooked complexity of Shakespeare's character and reflects a society struggling to reconcile art, nature, and the inevitability of decay.

In Millais' hands, Ophelia doesn't just die—she endures. Not in agony, but in the painted permanence of river-light, leaf-shadow, and an expression that dares us to look deeper.

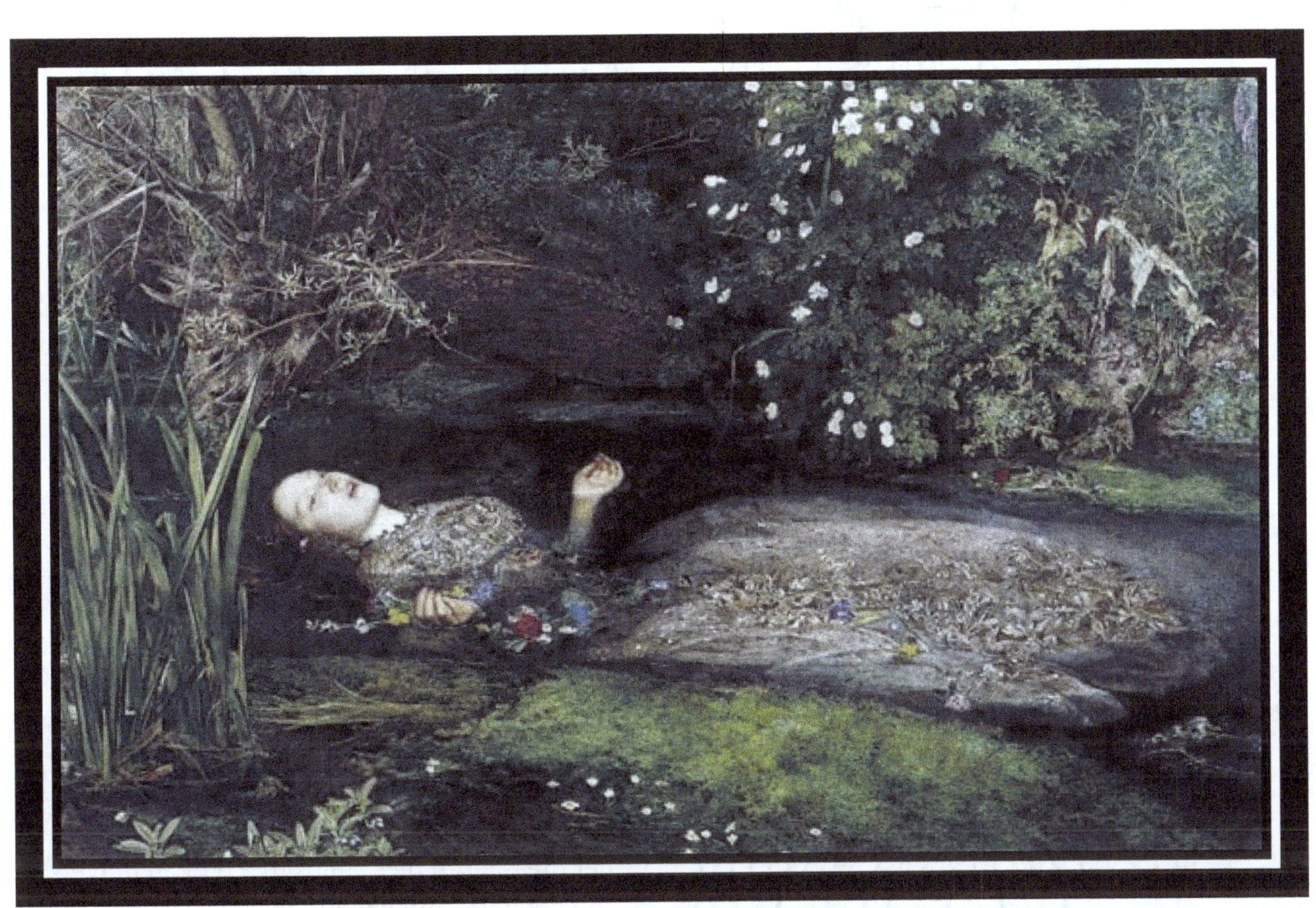

Ophelia (1851-2) by John Everett Millais

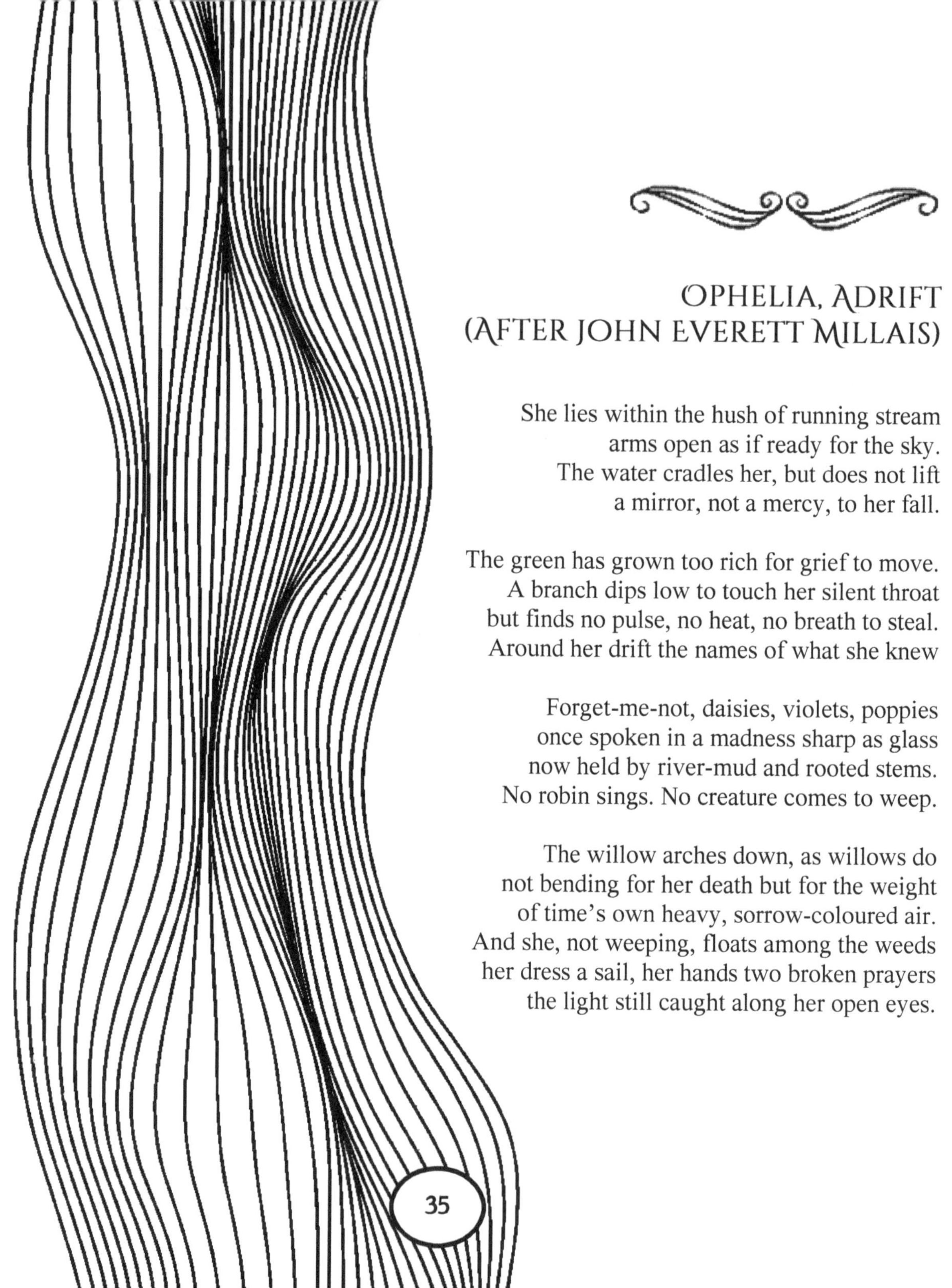

OPHELIA, ADRIFT
(AFTER JOHN EVERETT MILLAIS)

She lies within the hush of running stream
arms open as if ready for the sky.
The water cradles her, but does not lift
a mirror, not a mercy, to her fall.

The green has grown too rich for grief to move.
A branch dips low to touch her silent throat
but finds no pulse, no heat, no breath to steal.
Around her drift the names of what she knew

Forget-me-not, daisies, violets, poppies
once spoken in a madness sharp as glass
now held by river-mud and rooted stems.
No robin sings. No creature comes to weep.

The willow arches down, as willows do
not bending for her death but for the weight
of time's own heavy, sorrow-coloured air.
And she, not weeping, floats among the weeds
her dress a sail, her hands two broken prayers
the light still caught along her open eyes.

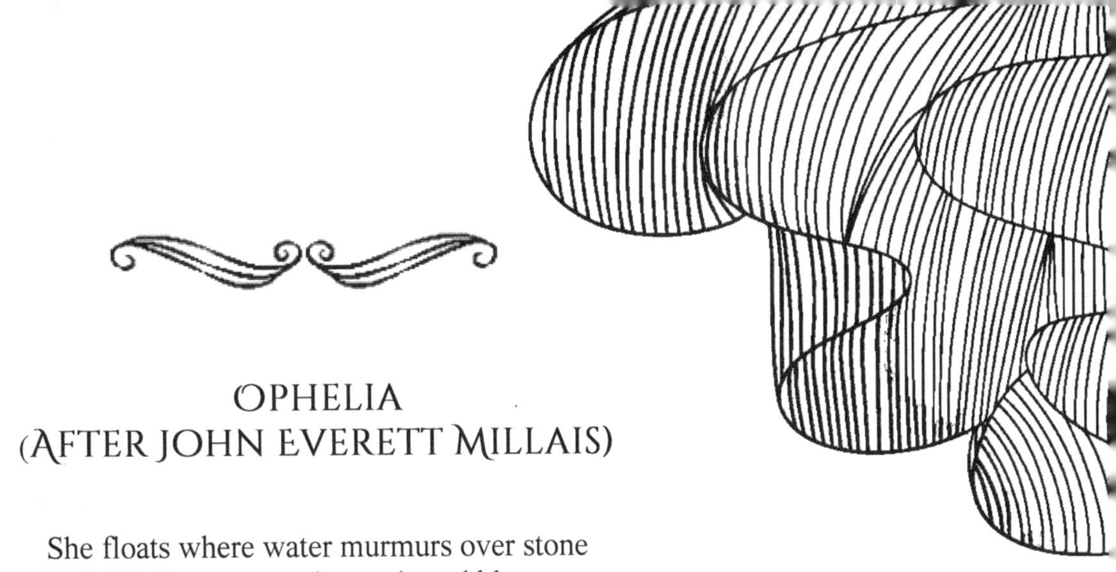

OPHELIA
(AFTER JOHN EVERETT MILLAIS)

She floats where water murmurs over stone
A lily lost among the reeds and bloom
Her fingers drift, their purpose overthrown
White hands resigned to nature's gentle tomb.

The flowers keep her memory in flame
Pale daisies, violets, and rue on shore
Each petal whispering her fading name
Adrift upon the stream she loved before.

No cry escapes her lips, though parted still
The willow leans, but does not touch her head.
The brook moves on, obeying its own will
It bears the living softly to the dead.

So beauty lingers where the heart has drowned
In silence deeper than the river's sound.

HAMLET UPON OPHELIA'S DEATH (AFTER JOHN EVERETT MILLAIS)

I loved thee once – nay, deeper than I dared
But madness wore the mask of my design.
Thy gentle soul was more than I declared
Yet met the edge of vengeance writ in mine.

I saw thee walk the edge of reason's wall
With flowers naming grief I could not stay.
Each step, a thread unravelled from thy fall
And I, too lost in rot to turn thy way.

Thy death is now the mirror to my guilt
Not drowned in brook, but in my broken vow.
My hands are clean, yet everything I've built
Has cast thee down to where I meet thee now.

If I had held thee closer in thy fright
Thou might'st have stayed to haunt me in the light.

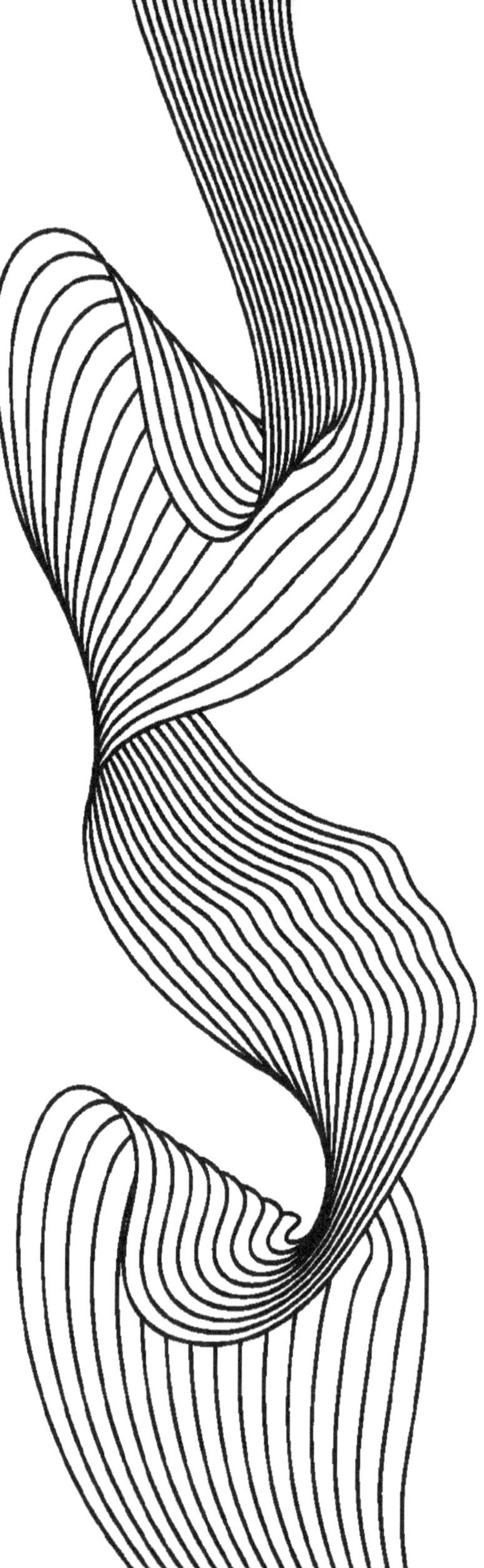

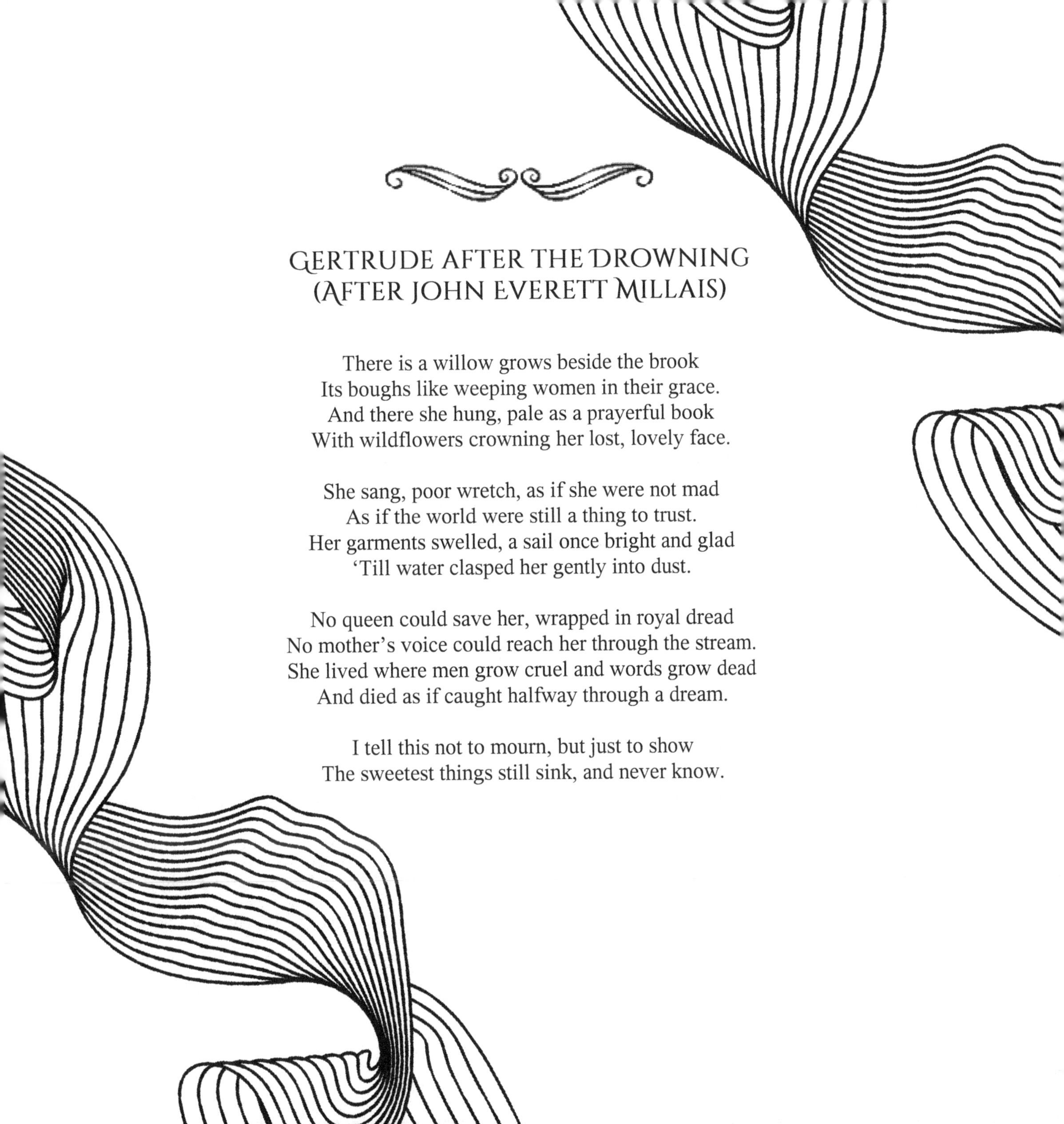

GERTRUDE AFTER THE DROWNING
(AFTER JOHN EVERETT MILLAIS)

There is a willow grows beside the brook
Its boughs like weeping women in their grace.
And there she hung, pale as a prayerful book
With wildflowers crowning her lost, lovely face.

She sang, poor wretch, as if she were not mad
As if the world were still a thing to trust.
Her garments swelled, a sail once bright and glad
'Till water clasped her gently into dust.

No queen could save her, wrapped in royal dread
No mother's voice could reach her through the stream.
She lived where men grow cruel and words grow dead
And died as if caught halfway through a dream.

I tell this not to mourn, but just to show
The sweetest things still sink, and never know.

BENEATH THE SURFACE

A FRESH LOOK AT DAVID HOCKNEY'S PORTRAIT OF AN ARTIST (POOL WITH TWO FIGURES)

Few paintings have captured the paradox of human connection and emotional distance quite like David Hockney's *Portrait of an Artist (Pool with Two Figures)*. Completed in 1972, this masterpiece straddles the lines between intimacy and alienation, clarity and ambiguity. At first glance, it might seem like a serene Californian day frozen in technicolour—two men, one submerged in crystal-clear water, the other standing clothed at the edge of the pool. But look closer, and the painting unfolds like a psychological drama set against the sun-drenched backdrop of Southern California.

A PAINTING BORN FROM LOSS AND OBSESSION

The story behind *Portrait of an Artist* is almost as compelling as the image itself. The figure standing at the pool's edge is Peter Schlesinger, Hockney's former lover and muse. The painting emerged from the wreckage of their romantic relationship—a love that had once burned brightly but ended with Hockney shattered. The swimmer is anonymous, face obscured by the surface of the water, adding a sense of mystery and perhaps even projection. Is this a ghost of Hockney's past? A stand-in for emotional detachment? Or is it simply a compositional foil to the standing figure?

The painting's genesis is famously unconventional. Hockney combined two unrelated photographs: one of a man swimming underwater, and another of someone standing and looking downward. The juxtaposition intrigued him—two figures in different planes of existence, separated by the refractive boundary of water. It took him months and multiple attempts to translate the concept into a coherent canvas. The final result is a masterclass in emotional tension and formal elegance.

STILLNESS IN MOTION

What makes *Portrait of an Artist* so uniquely captivating is its uncanny stillness. Everything in the scene is luminous and clear, almost hyperreal. The shadows are crisp, the pool tiles geometrically perfect, the water's ripples caught in a moment of impossible pause. Yet there's a powerful sense of unease. The standing figure gazes at the swimmer—not with affection, it seems, but with contemplation, maybe even accusation. There's no mutual gaze, no exchange. Only one sees; the other exists below, unseen.

This composition turns the viewer into a voyeur of an intensely private moment. Hockney offers no easy interpretations. Are we witnessing regret? A meditation on lost love? A metaphor for emotional depth and surface tension? The painting doesn't answer; it only asks.

THE LANGUAGE OF COLOUR AND FORM

One cannot discuss this painting without addressing Hockney's use of colour. His palette is all sun and clarity—turquoise blues, vivid greens, soft peach hues of skin and flesh. Yet the emotion is anything but light. There's a tension between the brightness of the scene and the heaviness beneath it, echoing the disconnect between exterior appearance and internal state. The water, meticulously rendered, acts as both a mirror and a barrier—a literal and figurative divide between worlds.

Architectural lines and geometric balance further ground the scene. The landscape's hills in the background evoke an Edenic tranquillity, but they're far away, unreachable. The tiled pool, meanwhile, is so precise it becomes a kind of emotional grid, placing its subjects in discrete compartments.

A TIMELESS MOMENT, ETERNALLY PAUSED

Though painted over half a century ago, *Portrait of an Artist (Pool with Two Figures)* continues to resonate. It's more than a portrait; it's an exploration of human relationships, of the things we see and the things we choose not to. In 2018, the painting shattered records, selling for over $90 million and becoming the most expensive work by a living artist at auction at the time. But its value lies far beyond its price tag.

In a world saturated with fleeting images and surface-level interactions, Hockney's painting demands pause. It invites reflection on the spaces we inhabit between closeness and distance, memory and reality. And perhaps most hauntingly, it reminds us that even under the clearest sky, what lies beneath the surface is never truly still.

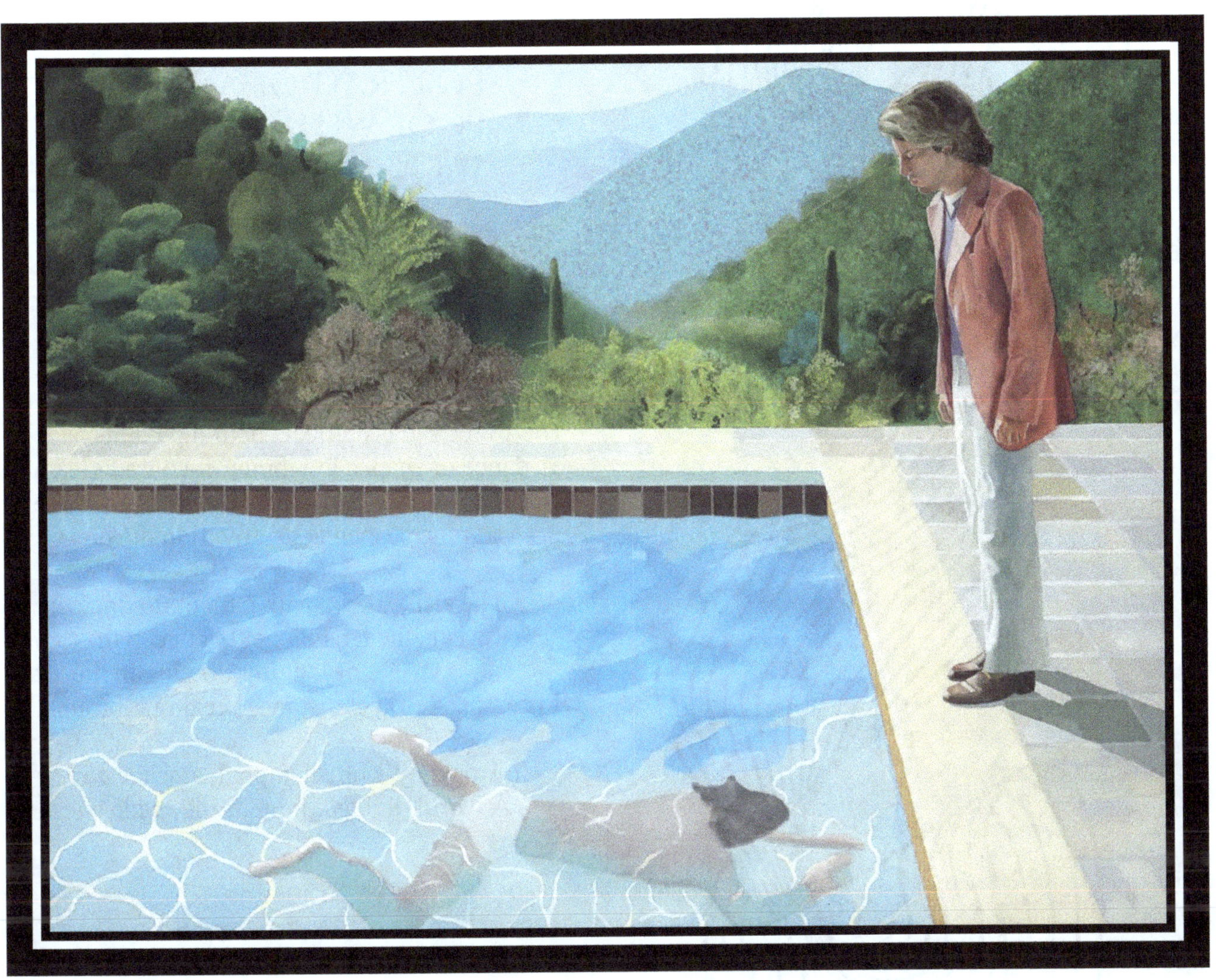

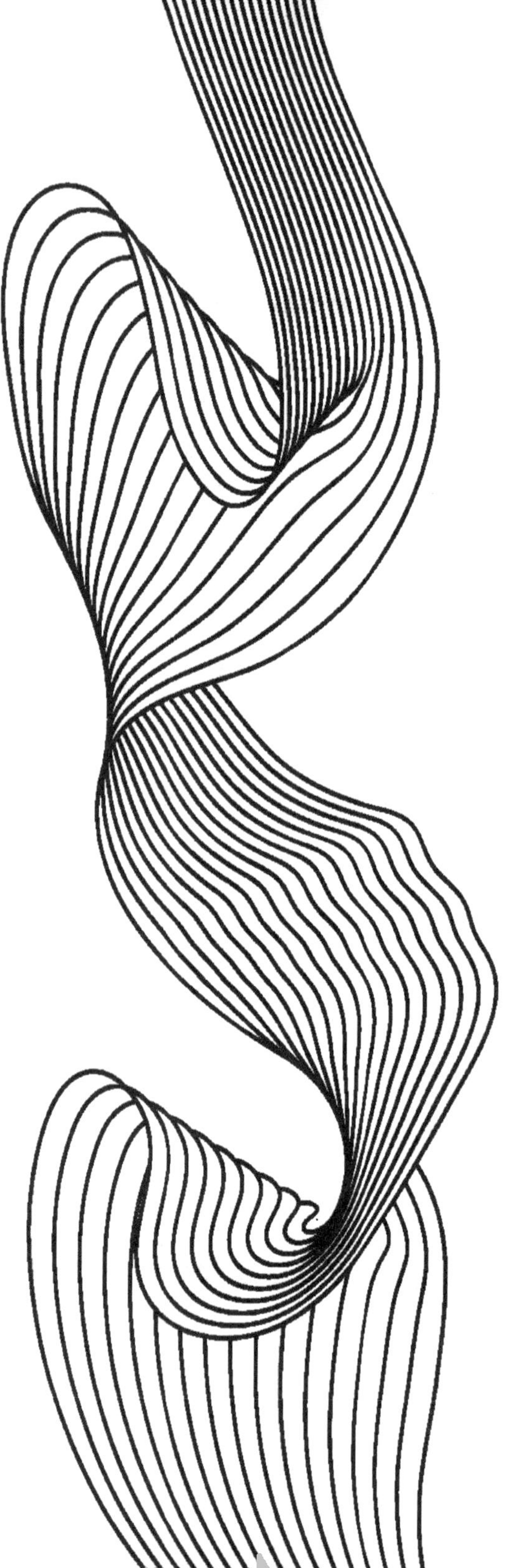

PORTRAIT OF AN ARTIST –
POOL WITH TWO FIGURES
(AFTER DAVID HOCKNEY)

Beneath the sun, a pool of crystal blue
Two figures poised, their worlds apart yet near
The swimmer dips in depths serene and true
While watcher stands, consumed by quiet fear.

The water's glass reflects both light and shade
A dance of shapes in vibrant, fractured gleam
Where silence hums and colours softly fade
And time suspends itself within the dream.

The artist's eye, with patient, loving care
Reveals the tension held between the two
A tale of longing floating in the air
Of presence felt, yet distance breaking through.

In Hockney's brush, a pool, a heart, a view
A world divided, joined, and made anew.

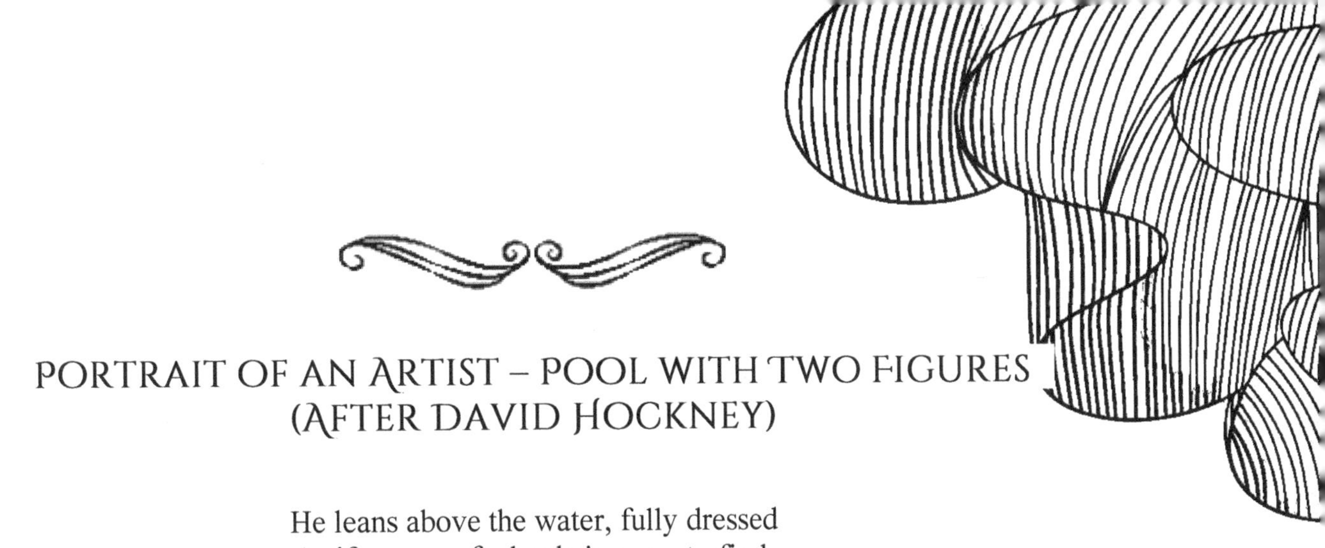

PORTRAIT OF AN ARTIST – POOL WITH TWO FIGURES
(AFTER DAVID HOCKNEY)

He leans above the water, fully dressed
As if unsure of what he's come to find.
The swimmer cuts a line through blue and glass
Unseen, or maybe choosing not to see.
Their bodies—one in motion, one in thought
Divide the canvas like a question asked
Too late to change the answer it implies.

The pool is still except where it is not
A shifting net of sunlight, fragments caught
In rippling patterns, clear but never still.
Behind them, hills roll back in silent pinks
Unbothered by the drama at the edge.
The scene is quiet—bright, and strangely still
But tension hums like something just submerged.

And though no words are spoken in the frame
The viewer feels the weight of things unsaid.
The swimmer swims. The standing figure waits.
The air between them holds the final brush.

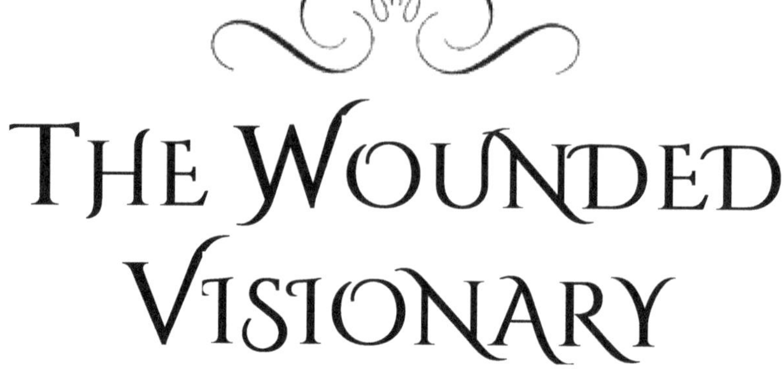

THE WOUNDED VISIONARY

A FRESH LOOK AT VAN GOGH'S SELF-PORTRAIT WITH BANDAGED EAR

Vincent van Gogh's *Self-Portrait with Bandaged Ear* is more than a painting—it is a haunting visual confession, an artistic act of resilience in the face of mental collapse. Painted in early 1889, shortly after the infamous incident in which Van Gogh severed part of his left ear – shown in the self-portrait as his right ear because he painted himself in a mirror. This work has come to symbolise the troubled genius of its creator. But beneath the familiar image lies a deeper narrative about identity, perception, and the uneasy relationship between suffering and creativity.

A PORTRAIT OF RECOVERY, NOT DESPAIR

Contrary to the popular romanticisation of Van Gogh as a tragic figure destroyed by his madness, *Self-Portrait with Bandaged Ear* offers a moment of quiet tenacity. The bandage, stark and white, wraps around the painter's head like both a wound and a halo. It marks a moment not of defeat but of continuation—he paints himself *after* the injury, not during. There's a certain defiance in this act, a refusal to let trauma erase him from his own story.

His face is pale, his expression subdued, and his eyes sidelong, avoiding direct confrontation with the viewer. Yet there's a calmness here too. Van Gogh dresses himself in a thick green overcoat, suggesting he is sheltering himself not just from the winter chill but from emotional exposure. Behind him, a Japanese print—a reference to the ukiyo-e art he adored—hangs on the wall, as if to anchor him to a world of idealised beauty even while his own spirals into chaos.

THE MIRROR'S TRUTH AND THE ARTIST'S LIE

One of the most intriguing elements of this painting is the reversal caused by the mirror. Van Gogh painted what he saw in reflection, so the bandage appears to be on the right ear—though we know he mutilated the left. This slight distortion opens a philosophical question: which self is real—the one the world sees, or the one the artist sees? In using the mirror to study himself, Van Gogh inadvertently reveals how fragile and subjective self-perception can be. The painting becomes less a record of a face and more a meditation on the fractured nature of identity.

THE SILENT DIALOGUE

Van Gogh often turned to self-portraiture in the absence of other models, but these works were never purely about likeness. In *Self-Portrait with Bandaged Ear*, the act of painting is itself therapeutic. It's as though he's trying to reconnect with himself through brush and pigment, to hold himself together with oil and canvas.

The presence of the Japanese print behind him isn't arbitrary. Van Gogh saw Japan as a land of purity and artistic enlightenment—a stark contrast to his inner turmoil. By placing this print in the composition, he establishes a silent dialogue between his own suffering and the serene ideal he aspired to. The contrast underscores the tension at the heart of the painting: the yearning for peace within a storm of the mind.

BEYOND THE MYTHS

It's easy to let the myth of Van Gogh—the tormented, unrecognised genius—overshadow the actual substance of his art. But to view *Self-Portrait with Bandaged Ear* solely as a symptom of illness is to miss its extraordinary clarity. The brushwork is deliberate, the colours controlled, the composition balanced. This is not the work of a man consumed by madness, but one who channels his vulnerability into a coherent and powerful artistic statement.

In today's conversations around mental health, Van Gogh's painting remains disarmingly relevant. It doesn't glamorise pain—it acknowledges it, confronts it, and dares to keep creating in spite of it. That quiet courage is what gives this painting its enduring impact.

WINDOW AND MIRROR

Self-Portrait with Bandaged Ear is not merely a window into Van Gogh's psyche; it's a mirror reflecting the complex nature of human endurance. Through his battered image, Van Gogh leaves us with something startlingly contemporary: a reminder that art is not born from suffering, but from the strength to face suffering with honesty and vision. In this portrait, Van Gogh is not just wounded—he is alive, alert, and, perhaps most poignantly, still painting.

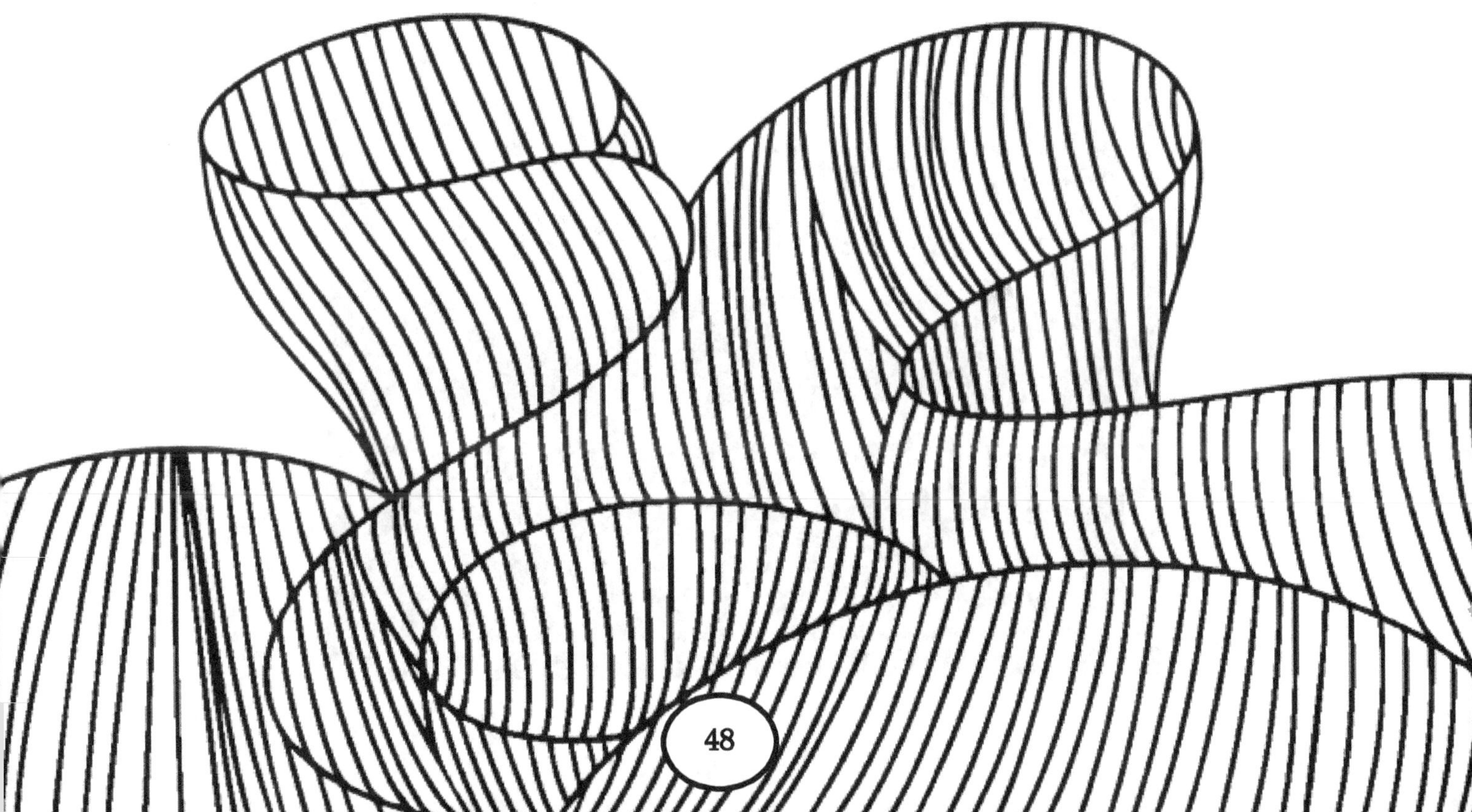

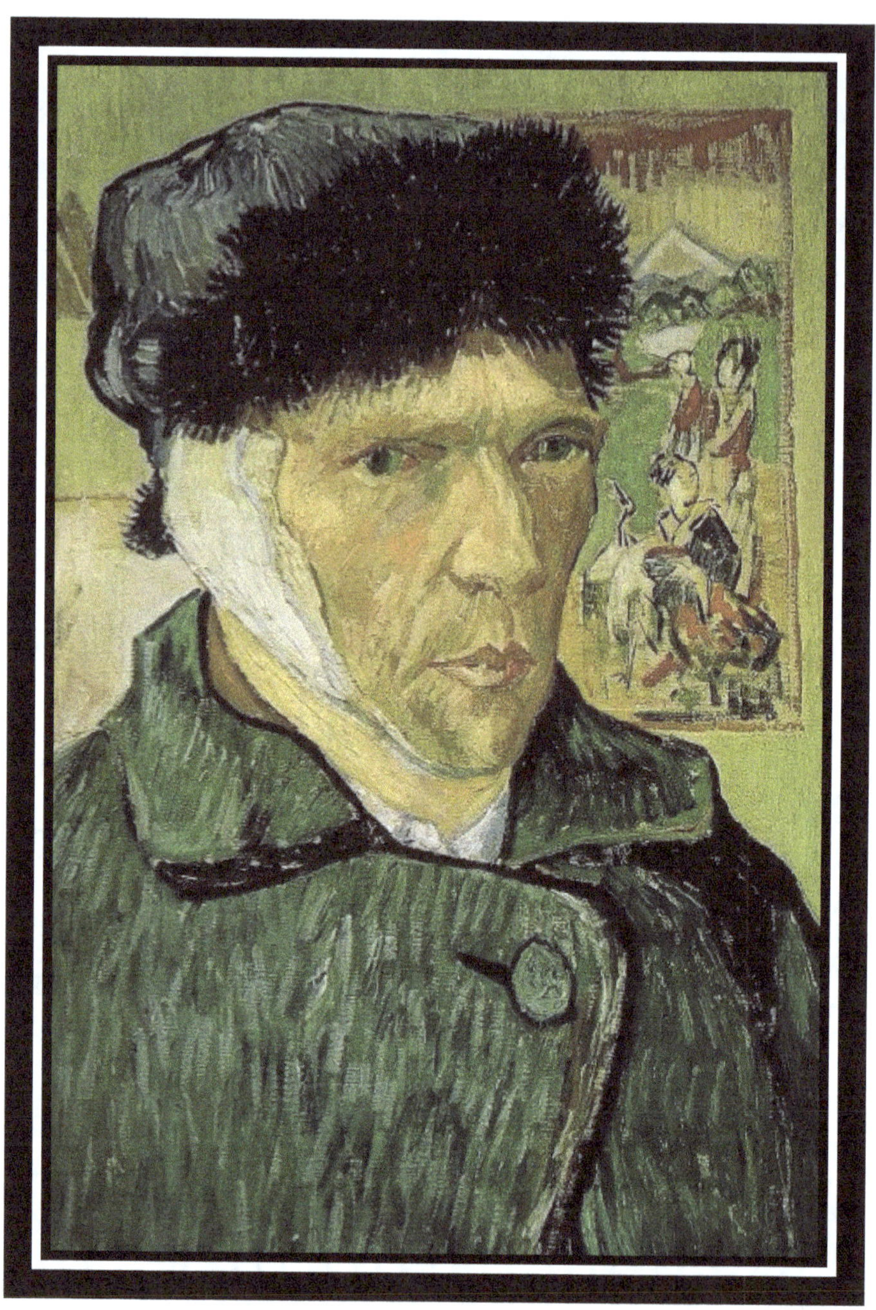

SELF-PORTRAIT WITH BANDAGED EAR

He sits beneath a shroud of muted light
The bandage wound where silence took its place.
His eyes, still burning, do not plead nor fight
But hold the haunted calm upon his face.

The coat hangs stiff – cool green recedes behind
While strokes of green and ochre pulse with flame.
No laughter lives within this painted day
Yet still he signs the work with his own name.

The pain is raw, yet pride outlives the blow
He paints not just the wound, but what remains
A man who let the inner tempest show
And turned his suffering into refrains.

Though blood was shed beneath that muted hue
He forged from loss a world more bright, more true.

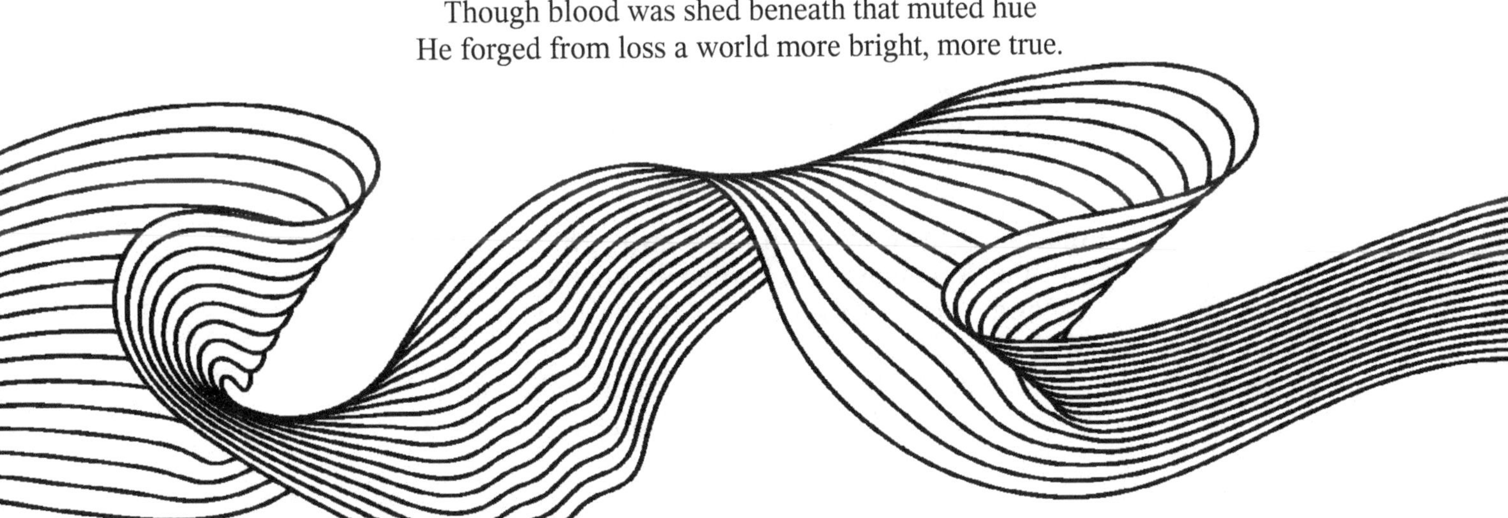

SELF-PORTRAIT WITH BANDAGED EAR
(AFTER VAN GOUGH)

He turns, half-shadowed, to the world bandaged a swath of gauze obvious on the wound
that coils like silence round the side of pain.
His eyes, unslept, are rivers rimmed with fire
yet fixed and still, as if to say, *I'm here*
though not the man you think, or want me to be.

The coat is green, the walls behind are green
the canvas hums with strokes that do not rest.
Each line declares a tremble in the soul
a hand that fought the frenzy of the light
and found, within its blaze, a kind of truth.
What truth? The ear is gone. The artist stays.

His lips are tight, resisting all regret.
No pity in that stare, no weak appeal.
He dares the eye to judge, yet will not plead
for what he's lost was never meant to last.
The world is brutal, but he met it full
with colour wielded like a blade of peace.

And though the wound still shows, wrapped and profound
the brush moves on, beyond the body's scream
toward beauty carved from all that would destroy.
So let him sit within this frame of dusk
a man who bled, and painted through the dark
and made his anguish holy in the hue.

TURBULENT TRANQUILITY

VAN GOGH'S STARRY NIGHT

Few paintings in the history of Western art have transcended time and genre as powerfully as Vincent van Gogh's *Starry Night*. It is more than just a nocturnal landscape — it is a fever dream on canvas, a swirling confession in oil paint that captures the psychic tempest of one of history's most enigmatic artists. Created in 1889 while Van Gogh was institutionalised in Saint-Rémy-de-Provence, this painting is often read as both a cry and a lullaby: a paradoxical meditation on chaos and serenity.

MORE THAN A NIGHT SKY

At first glance, *Starry Night* appears to be a simple rendering of a sleepy village under a bright, expressive sky. But the sky is alive — unnaturally so. It writhes, it pulses. Van Gogh doesn't paint the stars as fixed points of light; he gives them mass, gravity, and motion. The celestial bodies — exaggerated orbs glowing like electric embers — dominate the composition. They radiate energy, linking the heavens with the rolling hills and curling cypress trees below in a cosmic ballet of brushstrokes.

It is not a realistic depiction of night. In fact, the view Van Gogh painted didn't exist as seen. He pulled elements from memory, imagination, and observation, combining the factual and the fantastical. The village, for example, is a creative construct — perhaps more Dutch than French — a reflection of home remembered from afar.

A PORTRAIT OF THE ARTIST'S MIND

Much of *Starry Night*'s enduring power lies in the tension between calmness and agitation. The little town slumbers peacefully, its windows dark, its steeple standing tall in an otherwise horizontal composition. Above it, however, the sky is restless, almost violent. The contrast is jarring — and telling.

Van Gogh's mental health struggles are well-documented. During the time he painted *Starry Night*, he was recovering from one of his many psychological crises. In this context, the sky can be read as an echo of his inner world: uncontainable, electric, full of energy that can't be subdued. It is both beautiful and terrifying — like genius itself.

The great swirling vortex near the centre is a particular focal point. Some have interpreted it as a spiral galaxy, while others view it as a metaphor for emotional or spiritual turmoil. Either way, it serves as an axis around which the rest of the painting seems to turn, a visual representation of instability or transformation.

COLOUR AND MOTION AS EMOTION

Technically, the painting is a masterpiece of Post-Impressionist experimentation. Van Gogh rejects the quiet, dotted approach of pointillism in favour of long, muscular strokes. The brushwork is tactile and urgent — almost sculptural. The colours are bold: cobalt and ultramarine blues dominate, but they're pierced by the incandescent yellows and oranges of the stars and moon.

What's astonishing is how much motion Van Gogh packs into a still image. The painting doesn't just *show* the night — it *feels* like the night is moving around you. The atmosphere isn't passive; it presses in, envelops, and speaks.

BEYOND THE FRAME

Since its creation, *Starry Night* has become an icon — replicated, reinterpreted, and remixed endlessly in pop culture, design, and even tattoos. But this familiarity often obscures its strangeness, its revolutionary daring. In many ways, *Starry Night* anticipates the emotional abstraction of 20th-century art. It bridges the visible and invisible — offering a glimpse not just of the world outside, but of the universe within.

To see *Starry Night* is to look into Van Gogh's soul — or perhaps to catch a glimpse of your own. It is a night sky not as the eye sees it, but as the heart dreams it.

MIRROR FOR THE HUMAN CONDITION

Starry Night is more than one of the most famous paintings in the world. It is an act of radical emotional honesty, rendered in swirling paint. Van Gogh took the night — that universal symbol of mystery, solitude, and peace — and made it unquiet. In doing so, he created a mirror for the human condition: beautiful, turbulent, and full of stars.

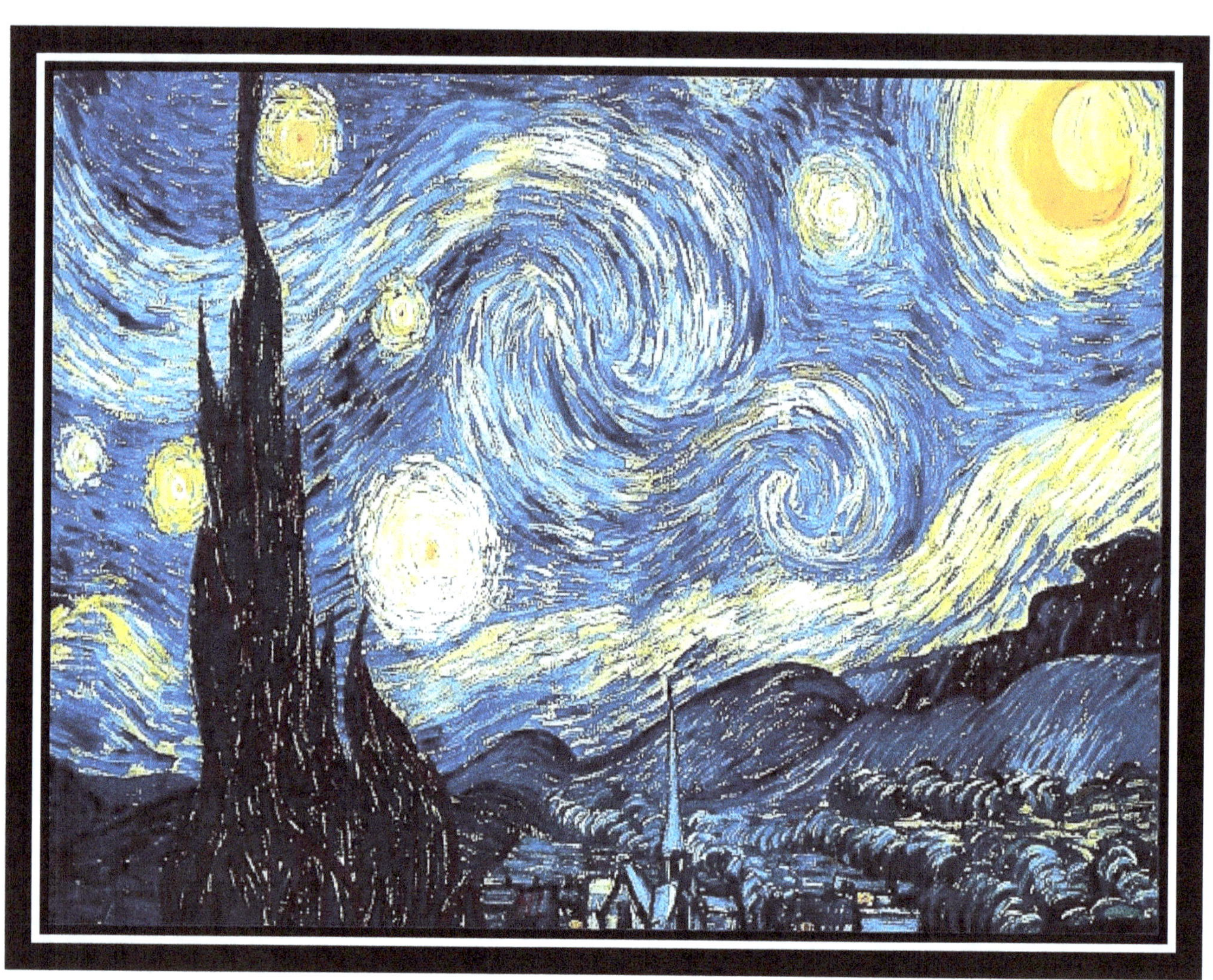

Starry Night by Vincent van Gogh

STARRY NIGHT

Above the roofs, the sky begins to spin
A whirl of stars in fevered, blazing flight.
They wheel like thoughts that storm the soul within
Unfolding flame across the throat of night.

The village sleeps, untouched by what you saw
Its quiet windows blind to fire and storm.
Yet in your eye, the sky defied all law
A living thing with pulse and breath and form.

The cypress reaches, rooted in the grave
Yet stretching toward the stars in black despair.
A flame of grief, too tall and wild to save
It splits the dark like unanswered prayer.

Though madness marked your hand and lit your frame
The world still turns beneath your burning name.

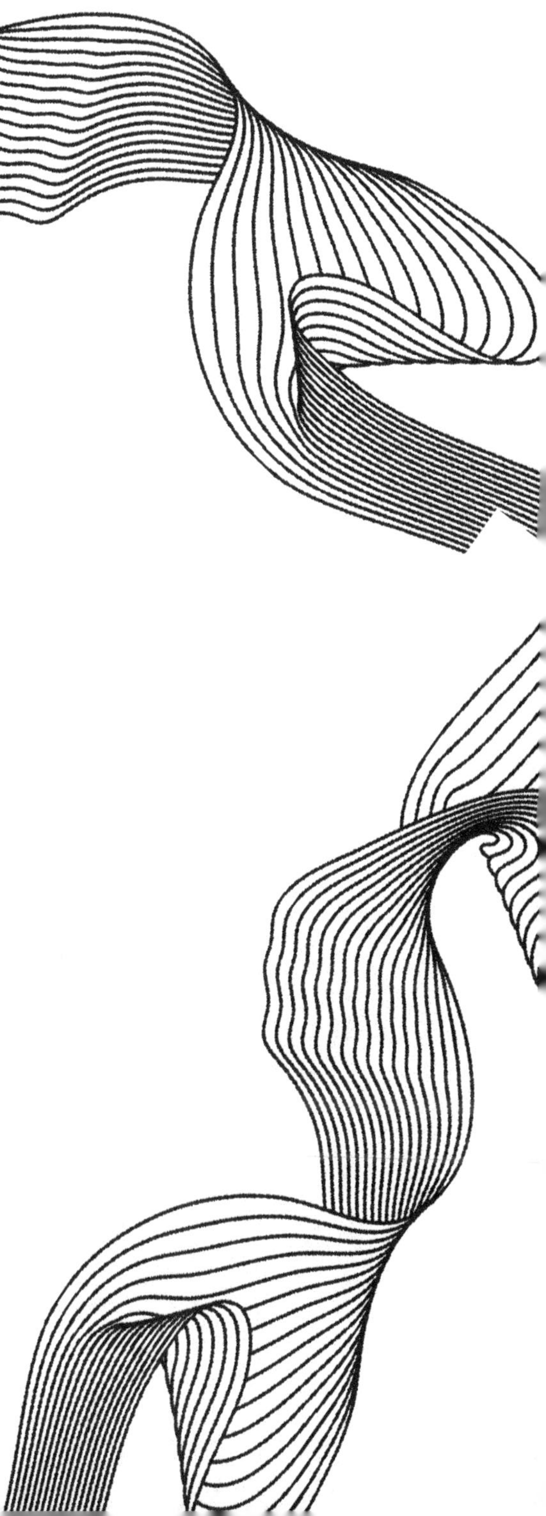

BENEATH THE STARRY NIGHT

No silence lies within this troubled sky
It hums with light the eye can barely hold.
The stars are wheels of fire, fierce and wide
That turn with purpose in the dark and cold.

The heavens twist in loops of sacred flame
As if the world above must speak, not rest.
Each swirl a cry, though no two speak the same
A burning sermon told without a crest.

Below, the village huddles in its sleep
Its houses small beneath the vast unknown.
No lamp within can match the dark so deep
Nor soothe the sky's relentless, star-wrought moan.

A cypress rises, black against the blue
A flame that climbs but never turns to ash.
It reaches where no human thought breaks through
A prayer in shape, a wound, a wordless lash.

And you, dear Vincent, locked behind your frame
What storm had passed to birth such blinding grace?
What sorrow shaped the stars and spoke your name
Then carved their ache across the sky's wide face?

Is this the cry of joy, or mad despair?
A world remade in strokes too wide to bind?

Or is it both—a vision born of care,
A soul unlatched and dancing through the mind?

The stars still turn, though you have turned to dust
And still the sky unfolds its burning truth.
It holds the weight of madness and of trust
The ancient ache you painted into proof.

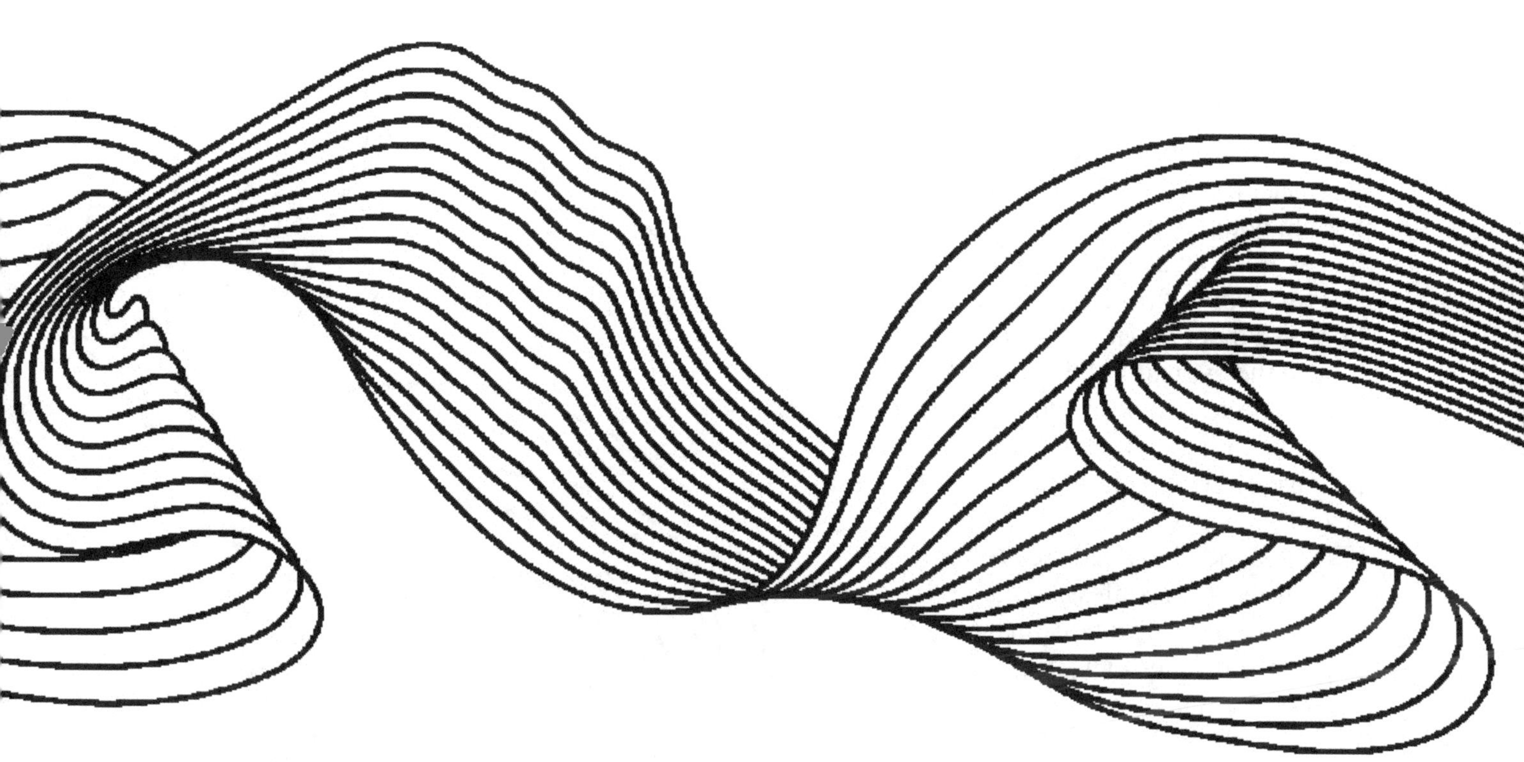

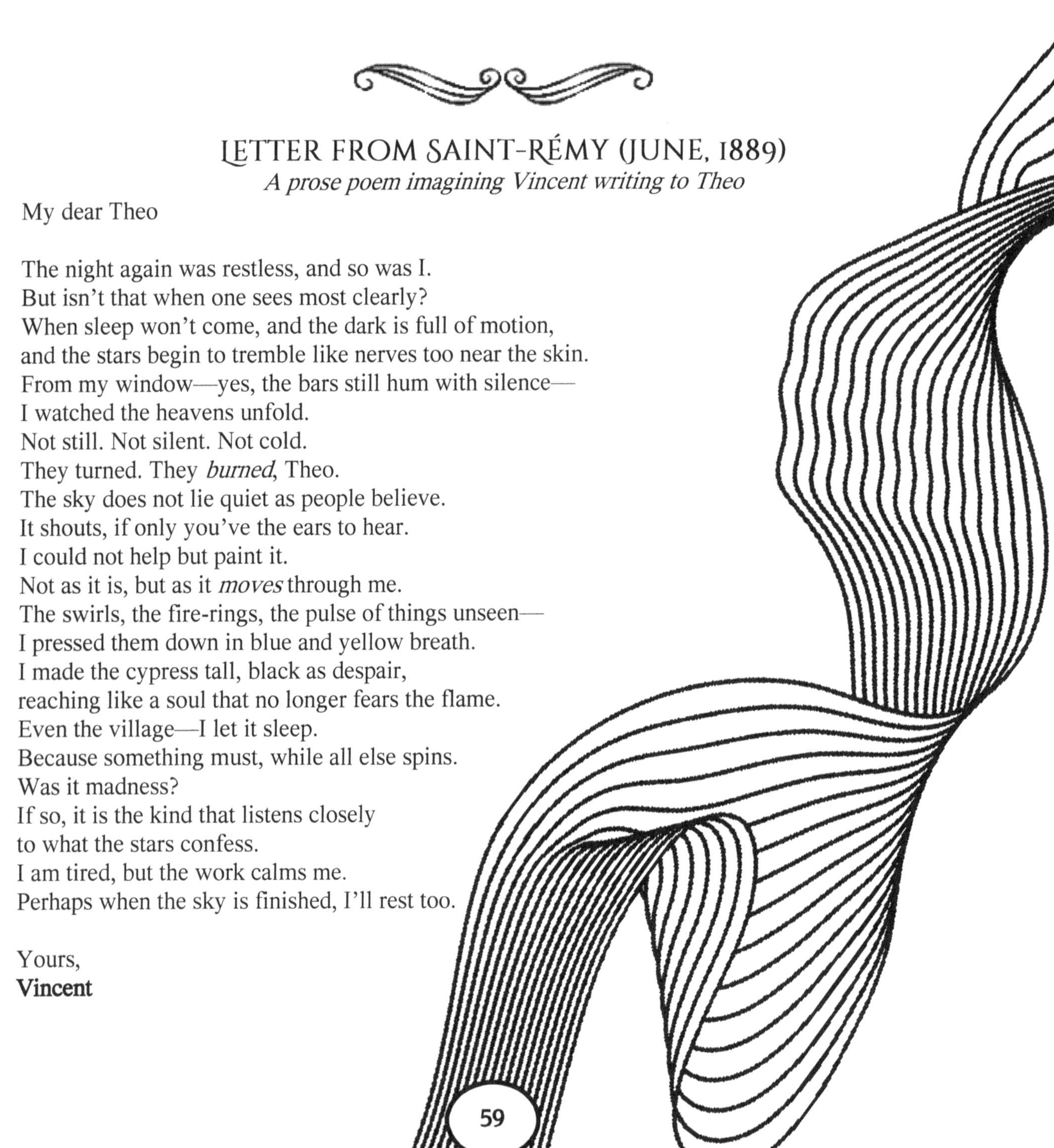

LETTER FROM SAINT-RÉMY (JUNE, 1889)
A prose poem imagining Vincent writing to Theo

My dear Theo

The night again was restless, and so was I.
But isn't that when one sees most clearly?
When sleep won't come, and the dark is full of motion,
and the stars begin to tremble like nerves too near the skin.
From my window—yes, the bars still hum with silence—
I watched the heavens unfold.
Not still. Not silent. Not cold.
They turned. They *burned*, Theo.
The sky does not lie quiet as people believe.
It shouts, if only you've the ears to hear.
I could not help but paint it.
Not as it is, but as it *moves* through me.
The swirls, the fire-rings, the pulse of things unseen—
I pressed them down in blue and yellow breath.
I made the cypress tall, black as despair,
reaching like a soul that no longer fears the flame.
Even the village—I let it sleep.
Because something must, while all else spins.
Was it madness?
If so, it is the kind that listens closely
to what the stars confess.
I am tired, but the work calms me.
Perhaps when the sky is finished, I'll rest too.

Yours,
Vincent

TAHITIAN WOMEN ON THE BEACH BY PAUL GAUGUIN

A WINDOW INTO PARADISE AND PARADOX

Paul Gauguin's *Tahitian Women on the Beach* (1891) is more than just an evocative scene from a faraway land — it is a masterwork that distils a complicated web of longing, colonialism, and aesthetic rebellion. Painted during his first sojourn in Tahiti, the artwork captures two women seated on the sand, their figures rendered with a calm dignity that reflects Gauguin's desire to escape the industrialised modern world in favour of something "primitive" and "pure." Yet beneath the canvas lies a layered narrative — one that complicates the tranquil surface with questions of identity, representation, and myth-making.

Aesthetic Simplicity – Symbolic Complexity

At first glance, *Tahitian Women on the Beach* is striking for its stillness. The composition is spare, the colour palette muted but warm. The women's postures are relaxed, and they seem both aware and unaware of the viewer — not quite subjects of a portrait, nor anonymous figures in a genre scene. Gauguin's use of broad planes of colour, unmodulated by traditional Western shading, evokes the influence of Japanese prints and cloisonnism[2], a technique that emphasises bold outlines and flat areas of pigment.

But simplicity is deceptive. The subtle, almost dreamlike tone of the work belies a deeper, more troubled cultural exchange. Gauguin did not paint Tahiti as it truly was — a colonised island shaped by French control and economic exploitation — but as he wished it to be: unspoiled, feminine, and spiritual. The women, in their quietude, are bearers of this fantasy.

The Myth of the Noble Savage

Gauguin arrived in Tahiti in 1891 disillusioned with the European art world. Seeking inspiration and a new kind of life, he imagined the South Pacific as a paradise beyond time — a place where, in his view, life was simpler and people more "authentic." This notion, of course, was a romantic distortion. His paintings from this period, *Tahitian Women on the Beach* among them, are steeped in the 19th-century myth of the "noble savage," which simultaneously exoticised and infantilised colonised peoples.

---

[2] **Cloisonnism** is a style of Post-Impressionist painting known for its use of vivid, flat colour blocks bordered by dark, typically black, lines. Inspired by the cloisonné enamel technique, this approach highlights simplified shapes and striking colour contrasts, often foregoing intricate detail and realistic perspective to produce a decorative effect similar to stained glass.

In the painting, the women are portrayed with dignity, but they are also silent and passive — as if their entire presence is in service to Gauguin's gaze. They become aesthetic objects, ideals rather than individuals. This duality — reverence mixed with objectification — runs through much of Gauguin's Tahitian work.

A MODERNIST REBELLION

Despite the problematic implications of Gauguin's vision, *Tahitian Women on the Beach* marks a radical break from the conventions of European painting at the time. It is part of a larger modernist impulse to challenge realism, linear perspective, and academic technique. Gauguin's move toward symbolic expression, flattened space, and emotional colour was foundational for later developments in Expressionism and Primitivism.

The painting's lack of narrative or dramatic action suggests a moment outside of time — an effect that resonated with the Symbolist movement, which sought to convey the ineffable and the eternal. In that sense, *Tahitian Women on the Beach* is less about ethnography than metaphysics. It seeks not to document reality but to conjure a feeling — of solitude, of longing, of the eternal feminine.

A CONTESTED LEGACY

Today, Gauguin's work invites both admiration and critique. His ability to reshape painting — to infuse it with personal myth and emotional abstraction — is undeniable. Yet so too is the ethical tension that underpins his representations of Polynesia. *Tahitian Women on the Beach*, like much of his oeuvre, straddles this divide: it is both beautiful and troubling, poetic and political.

To view it is to confront a contradiction — the desire to escape a broken world by constructing an idealised other, and the costs that come with that construction. Gauguin gave form to a dream, but the dream, like all dreams, reveals more about the dreamer than the world he imagines.

In the still sands of Tahiti, Gauguin found both inspiration and illusion. His women on the beach sit quietly, caught between the truth of their land and the fantasy of the man who painted them.

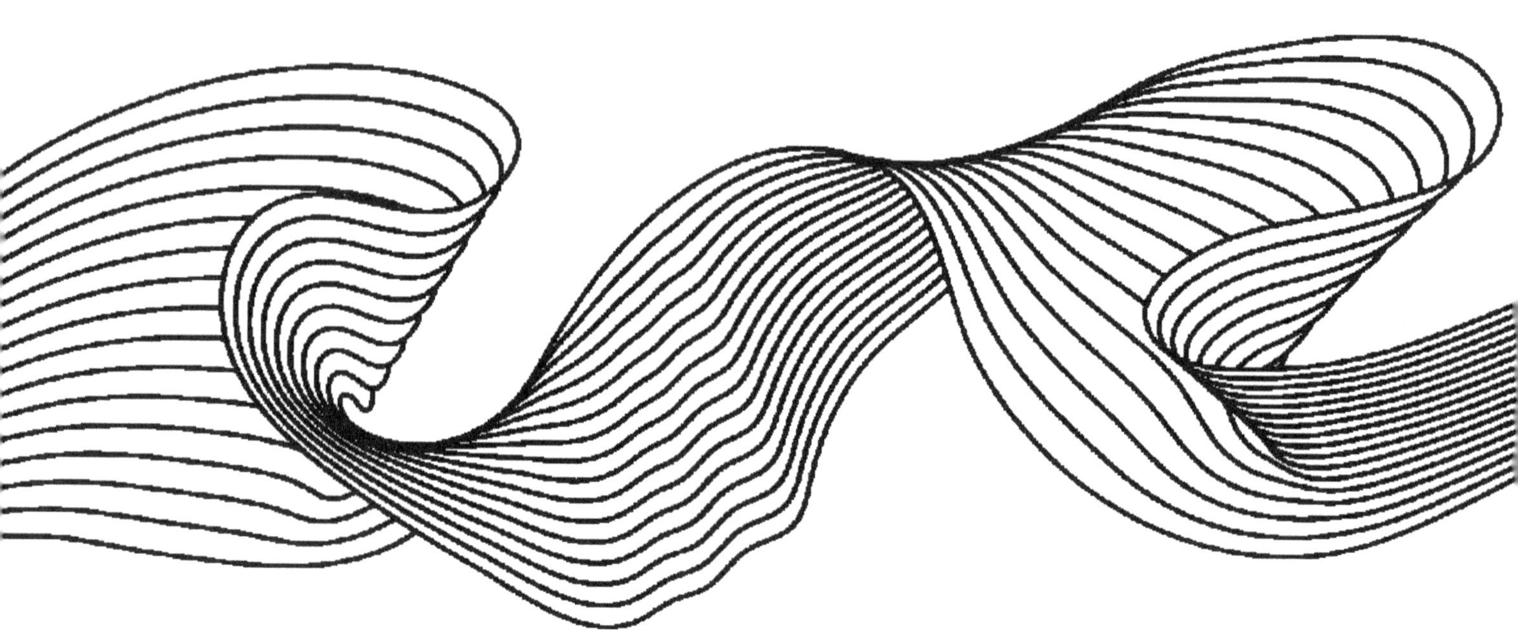

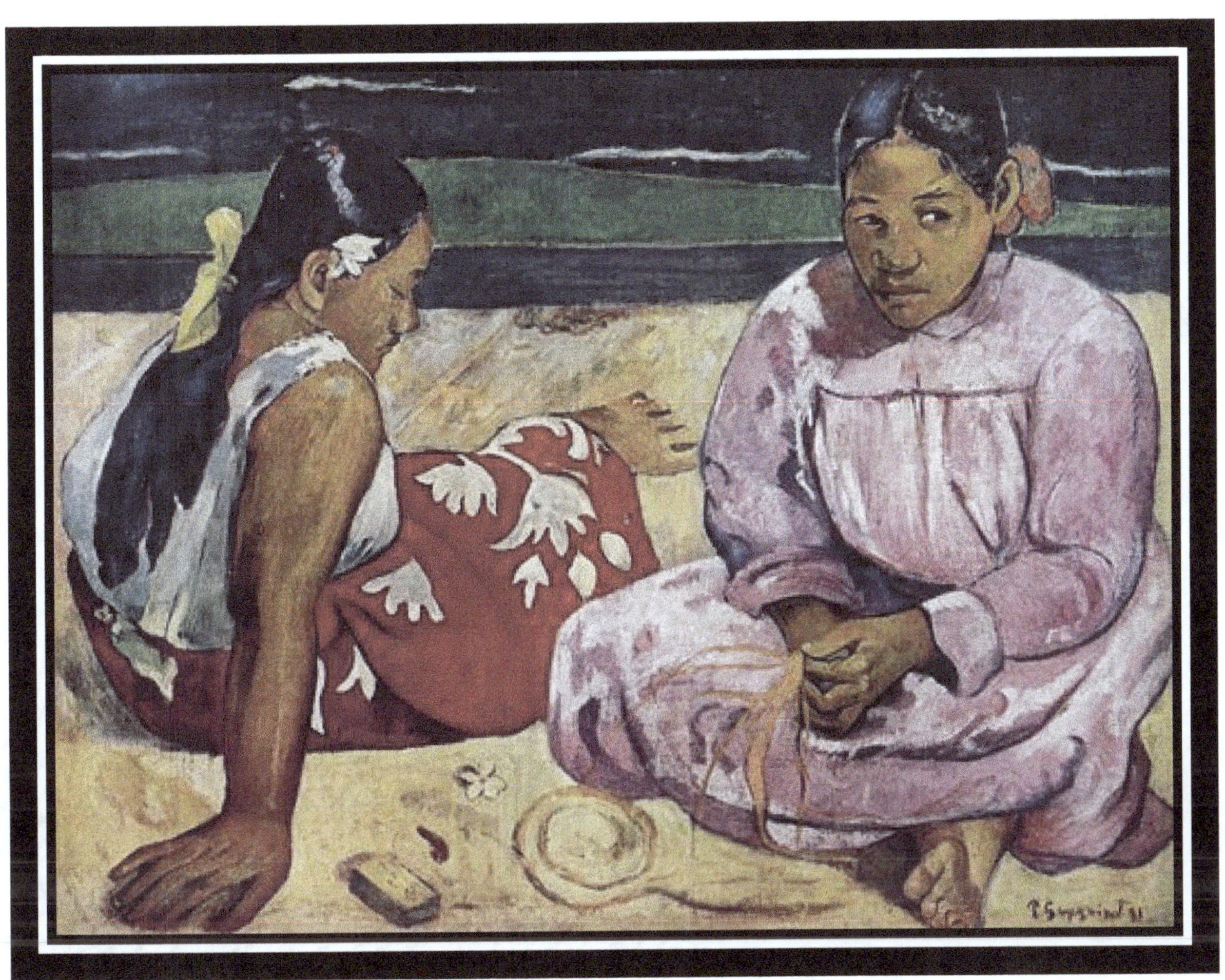

TAHITIAN WOMEN ON THE BEACH
(AFTER GAUGUIN)

No sky above, just earth and muted sea
Two women rest where silence folds the day.
The sand is warm with time's simplicity
Their gazes turned in thought or far away.

One leans upon her hand in soft repose
The other, still, as if she hears a sound
Some island voice the painted moment knows
Held deep within the hush of sacred ground.

No gesture forced, no posture made for show
They sit like myths that breathe in human clay.
The earth around them pulses soft and low
Its colour rich as dusk that will not stray.

What lives in them escapes the artist's frame
Yet in his brush, they live without a name.

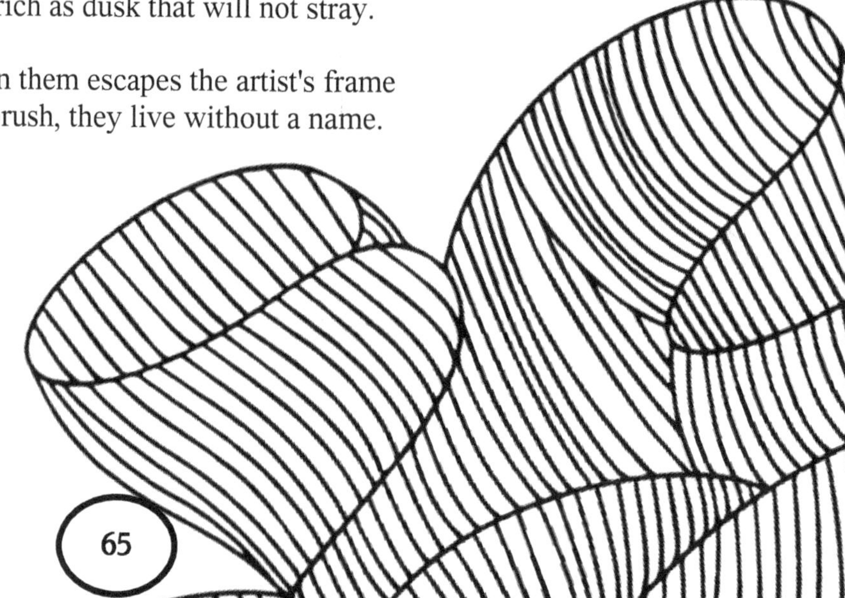

TAHITIAN WOMEN ON THE BEACH
(AFTER GAUGUIN)

They sit in sand that holds the warmth of day
Their bodies still, yet filled with inner tide.
No sky surrounds them—only earth and sea
A world enclosed in ochre, rust, and green.
The ocean waits beyond, a silent breath
Its shimmer hinted at in curling waves.

One gazes out, her posture eased by thought
A dreamer sunk in rhythms of the shore.
The other turns, her body half in pause
As if she hears a voice just out of reach
Not ours, but born of mango trees and stone
Of ancient chants that linger in the air.

Their limbs are bare, yet dignified with ease
Not posed, but resting in a truth they know.
Around them lies the hush of island time
Where nothing begs to move before it must.
Their silence speaks of things not said in words
A sisterhood of sun and salted wind
Of toil and rest, of ritual and soil.

The earth, thick-red and golden in its sleep
Surrounds them like a cradle, deep and wide.
No sky intrudes to break the bounded scene
No drifting cloud distracts from what is here

The curve of hip, the slope of neck and back
The fabric fallen loosely at their sides.

What Gauguin saw was not just form and hue
But myth made flesh, a stillness made to last
As if these women, in their grounded grace
Could hold the meaning of the land itself.
And we, who gaze through oil and time and glass
Are left to wonder what remains unseen
And who they were before the brush arrived.

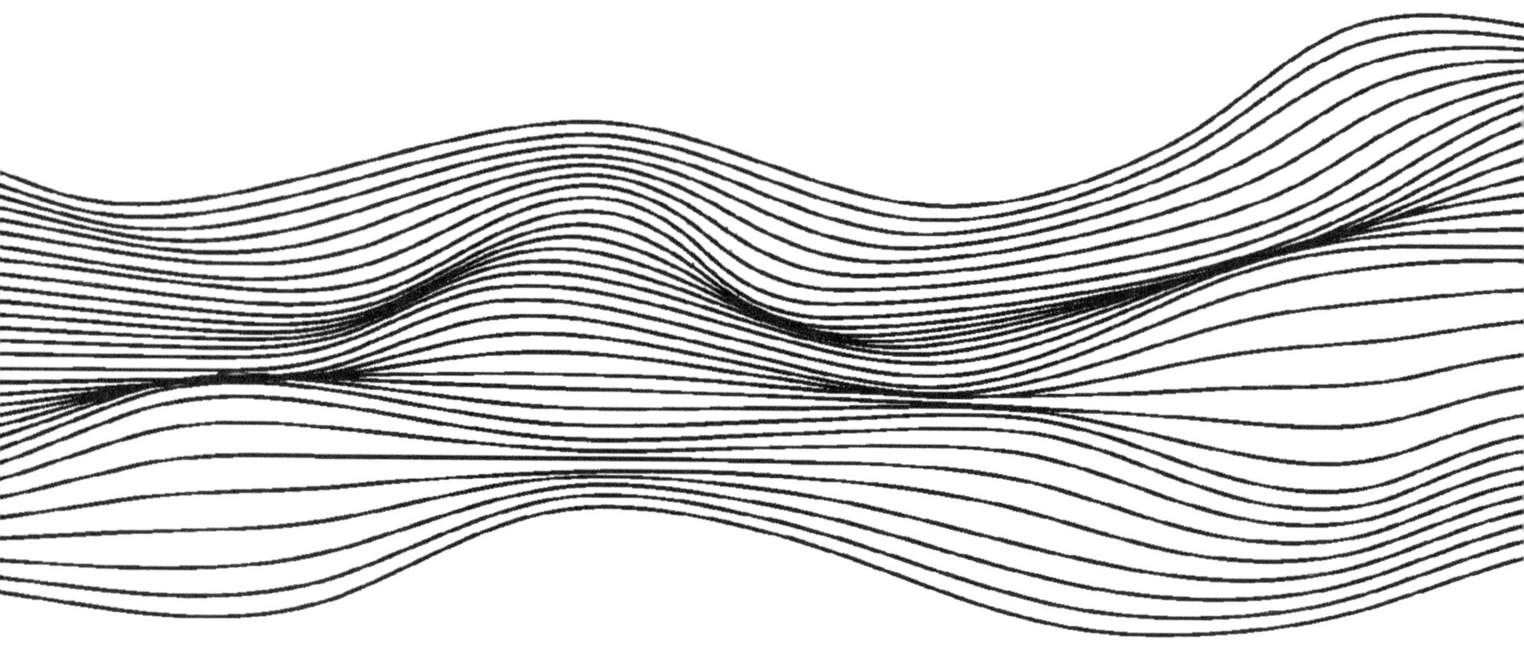

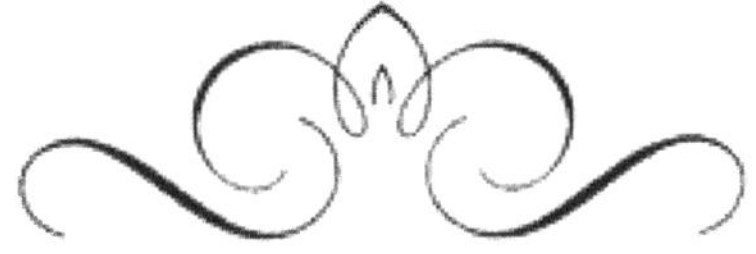

THE BIRTH OF VENUS

BOTTICELLI'S ETHEREAL MASTERPIECE AND THE REBIRTH OF BEAUTY

In the realm of Renaissance art, few images are as immediately iconic as *The Birth of Venus* by Sandro Botticelli. Painted around 1485–1486, this enchanting work transcends its era, whispering of myth, sensuality, and humanist ideals all at once. More than just a depiction of a mythological tale, Botticelli's Venus is a meditation on beauty's divine origin and its ability to awaken the soul.

A NEW KIND OF VENUS

Unlike earlier representations of the goddess of love, Botticelli's Venus is not sculpted in marble or swathed in rich textures. She emerges, instead, from the sea upon a giant scallop shell, her body pale and elongated, a study in elegant restraint. Her pose—demure, yet confident—borrows from classical statuary but softens the contrapposto[3] into something more dreamlike. This isn't the

---

[3] **Contrapposto** – is a pose of the human body where the arms and shoulders are positioned differently from the hips and legs, creating a contrasting yet balanced arrangement.

robust sensuality of a Titian nude; Botticelli's Venus is all breath and breeze, a figure of idealised love rather than carnal reality.

A POETIC MYTHOLOGY

The painting draws from the myth of Venus's birth, as told by ancient poets like Hesiod and later romanticised in Renaissance interpretations. According to legend, Venus (or Aphrodite) was born from the sea foam after the god Uranus was castrated and his blood fertilised the ocean. Botticelli's vision, however, sidesteps the more brutal origins of the myth in favour of an ethereal moment: the goddess arriving at the shore, gently propelled by Zephyrus—the god of the west wind—and his consort Chloris, while a Hora[4] of spring waits to clothe her.

This mythological tableau is steeped in symbolism. Zephyrus's[5] breath represents divine inspiration, the shell is a symbol of feminine birth and purity, and the waiting figure with a billowing floral robe offers the transition from divine nudity to civilised beauty. Botticelli's Venus is not just being born from the sea—she's being born into culture, into the aesthetic values of Florence's Neo-Platonic circle.

HUMANISM IN PAINT

The intellectual soil that nourished *The Birth of Venus* was the Florentine court of Lorenzo de' Medici, where classical learning mingled with Christian spirituality and artistic ambition.

---

[4] Hora is one of the three Horae, also known as the Hours—minor Greek goddesses who represent the seasons and divisions of time, and who often accompany Venus. The flowers adorning her dress hint that she symbolises the Hora of Spring. Like Venus, she stands in a contrapposto pose, appearing calm and joyful in response to Venus's arrival.
[5] In Greek mythology, Zephyrus represents the west wind and is commonly portrayed as a mild and benevolent breeze. As one of the four Anemoi, or wind deities, he is linked to the arrival of spring, the renewal of life, and fertility.

Botticelli, working in this atmosphere, painted not merely to adorn walls, but to stimulate thought. His Venus may be mythological, but she is also a visual allegory for divine love, an embodiment of the soul's ascent toward the ideal.

This philosophical underpinning was shaped by thinkers like Marsilio Ficino, who translated Plato's writings and proposed that beauty on Earth was a reflection of divine perfection. Viewed in this light, Venus's calm demeanour and radiant grace become expressions of a higher truth—beauty not as temptation, but as a gateway to the divine.

THE DELIBERATE FANTASY

Stylistically, Botticelli's painting is marked by a deliberate departure from naturalism. The sea's ripples are stylised rather than realistic, the figures float more than stand, and the anatomy, while graceful, is idealised. This departure from the physical world serves a purpose: Botticelli isn't trying to mimic life, but to elevate it. He invites viewers into a poetic space where nature, myth, and spirit blend seamlessly.

This is especially evident in the linear rhythms of the painting—the flowing hair of Venus, the fluttering robes, the curve of the shell—all drawn with a lyrical finesse that seems more attuned to music or verse than visual reality. It's as if Botticelli is painting not what he sees, but what he imagines beauty to be.

Although Botticelli's fame faded somewhat after his death, *The Birth of Venus* has enjoyed a profound modern revival. In the 19th and 20th centuries, it was embraced by the Pre-Raphaelites and Symbolists for its spiritual sensuality. In the age of pop culture, it has been endlessly reproduced, parodied, and referenced—from fashion to film.

But despite its ubiquity, the painting retains its mystery. Venus's gaze, calm and ambiguous, still holds a power that defies easy interpretation. Is she aware of her divine role? Is she modest, indifferent, or knowingly seductive? Botticelli leaves these questions open and perhaps it is this ambiguity that continues to captivate us.

MORE THAN A GODDESS

The Birth of Venus is more than a portrayal of a goddess—it is a manifesto of Renaissance ideals, a visual poem about the soul's yearning for beauty, harmony, and transcendence. In Botticelli's hands, myth becomes metaphor, and the nude becomes noble. Venus does not merely arrive on a shell; she arrives in our imagination, eternal and ever-renewing.

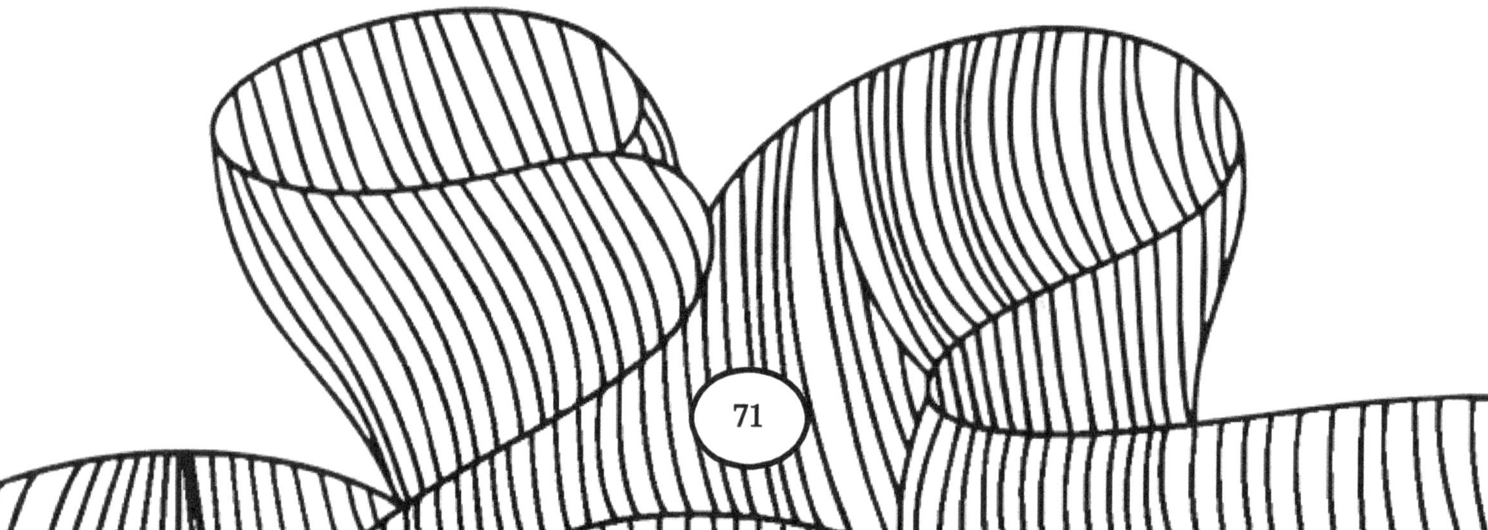

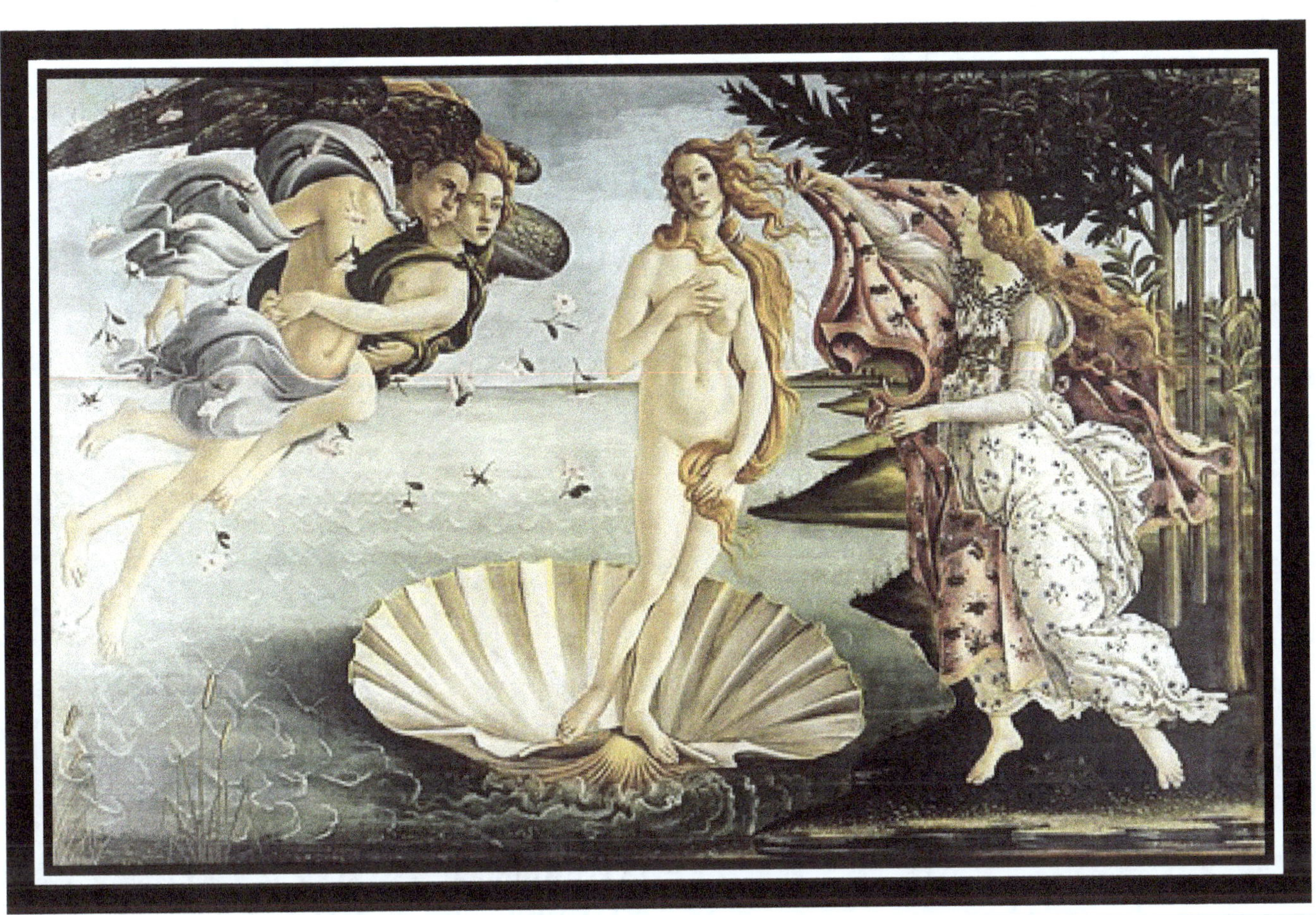

THE BIRTH OF VENUS
(AFTER BOTTICELLI)

Upon the sea's soft breath she rises fair,
A goddess born from foam and morning light,
Her golden hair cascades beyond compare
A vision clothed in dawn's first gentle bright.

The winds caress her skin with tender grace
While Zephyr's breath ignites the rose's bloom
She stands adorned in beauty's perfect place
A shell her throne, emerging from the gloom.

No mortal hand could craft such form divine
No human heart contain such calm and fire
Between the sea and sky her lights entwine
Awakening the world's unspoken choir.

O Venus, born of waves and whispered dreams
You bring to life the world with endless gleams.

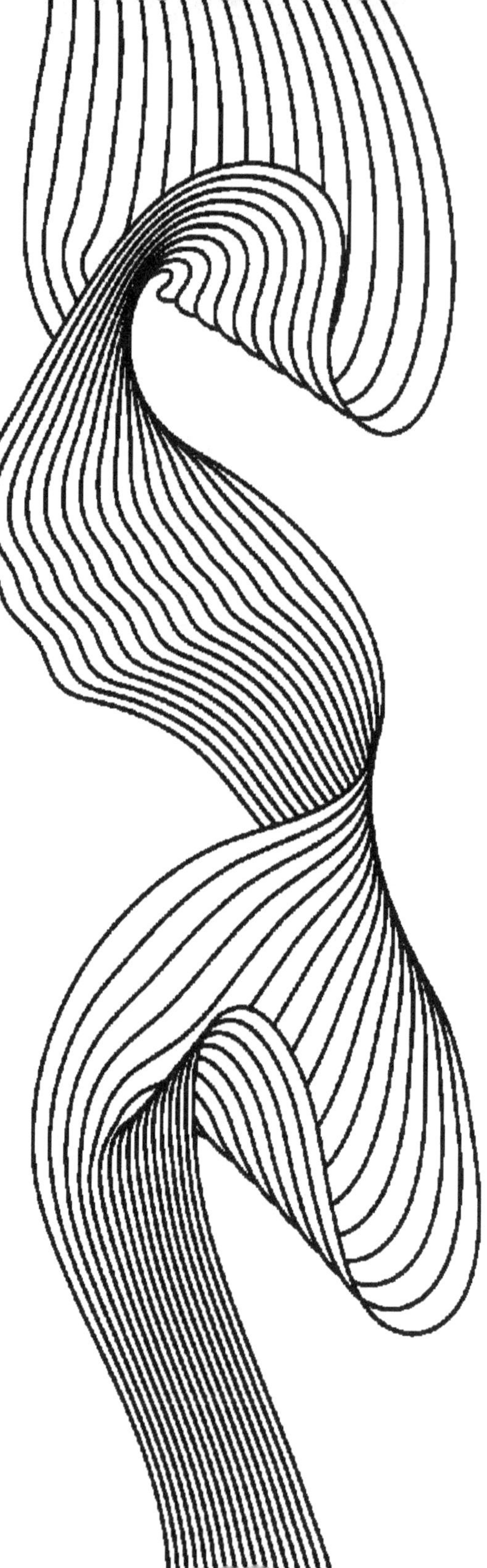

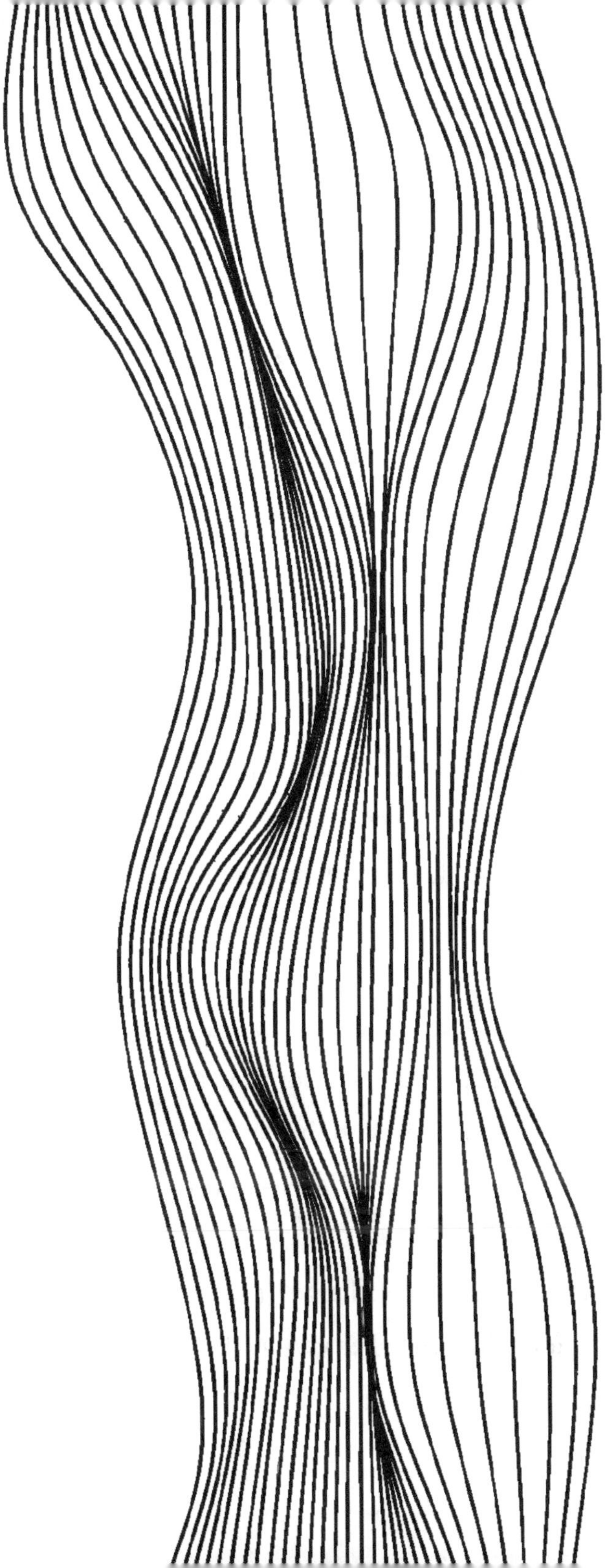

THE BIRTH OF VENUS
(AFTER BOTTICELLI)

She rises from the sea, a bloom of light
As foam dissolves along the curling tide.
The winds lean close, their cheeks with tender breath
To ferry her on petals, pale and wide.

No shell has held such beauty in its curve
No sky has arched so gently overhead.
The air is touched with gold, as Zephyrus
And Chloris guide her with a softened gale.

A goddess formed from sea and dream and grace—
Not flesh, but form that answers to the soul
She stands unarmed, yet all the world disarmed
Her gaze both innocent and infinite.

To shore she moves, the flowers at her feet
As Horae waits with cloak of spring in hand
To veil what none can name, yet all revere.
The world begins anew with every step.

Here art becomes a mirror for the gods
And beauty stands where time itself holds breath.

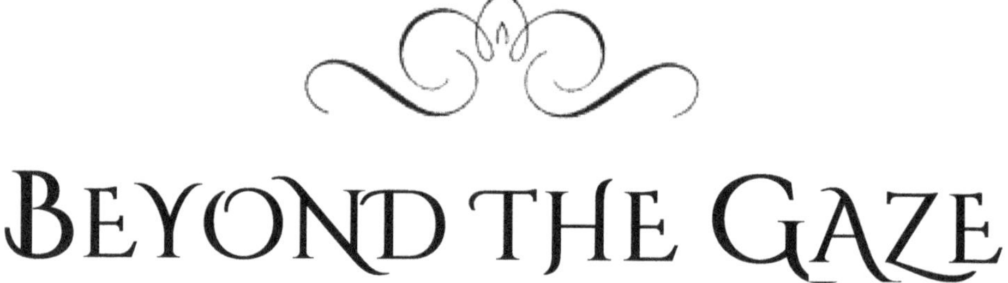

BEYOND THE GAZE

REIMAGINING VERMEER'S GIRL WITH A PEARL EARRING

Johannes Vermeer's *Girl with a Pearl Earring* (c. 1665) has been endlessly admired, analysed, and replicated—an enigmatic fragment of the Dutch Golden Age that has transcended its canvas to become a cultural icon. Often dubbed the "Mona Lisa of the North," this painting has been both celebrated and mystified. Yet beneath the surface of soft brushwork and luminous skin lies a quiet power often overlooked: the painting is not merely a portrait of a girl, but a moment suspended—fragile, cinematic, and hauntingly human.

A STUDY IN STILLNESS AND SUSPENSE

Unlike many of Vermeer's more domestic, narrative-rich scenes, *Girl with a Pearl Earring* is starkly simple. There is no background to interpret, no household object to anchor us in the rhythms of 17th-century life. The girl turns her head toward the viewer, lips slightly parted, as though interrupted or caught mid-thought. Her wide eyes hold something just out of reach—an emotion too delicate to name.

This ambiguity is precisely what grants the painting its emotional charge. It feels less like a static portrait and more like a fleeting encounter—one you might remember vividly, but only for a moment. The lack of detail in her environment emphasises her aliveness; she emerges from shadow into light with such subtlety that she seems almost real.

WHO IS SHE? THE UNANSWERED QUESTION

Historians have long debated the identity of the girl. Is she Vermeer's daughter? A servant? A model imagined rather than known? Theories abound, yet no documentation confirms her existence. Unlike his other known sitters—usually women engrossed in reading, music, or letter-writing—this girl does not act. She simply is.

By placing her outside any discernible context, Vermeer invites the viewer into a unique kind of intimacy. She is not a subject with a story but an image of quiet sensation. Her lack of identity becomes her strength: she becomes universal, timeless—a figure on the edge of becoming someone, or slipping away.

THE PEARL THAT ISN'T

A curious feature of the painting is the titular pearl itself. Scholars have noted that the earring seems unrealistically large and perhaps even painted without precise form or reflection. Some have argued that it may not be a pearl at all, but rather a reflective glass or imagined bauble. Whether illusion or embellishment, the pearl serves as the painting's visual fulcrum—a counterweight to her gaze, catching light as her eyes catch ours.

In many ways, the pearl mirrors the nature of the painting itself: luminous, ambiguous, and mysterious in its simplicity. It hangs improbably, like a question that will never fully resolve.

A PORTRAIT OF IMAGINATION

More than a portrait, *Girl with a Pearl Earring* feels like a metaphor for art's power to evoke what cannot be fully named. Her expression is not dramatic or overt—it's a whisper rather than a declaration. Yet that whisper echoes across centuries.

Vermeer's mastery lies not just in technique, but in restraint. The subtle gradations of light, the soft curve of her lips, the sheen of her turban—all converge not to tell a story, but to evoke a presence. She is an embodiment of stillness and suggestion.

CULTURAL AFTERLIFE

The painting's modern fame owes as much to its mystery as to its aesthetics. It has inspired novels, films, fashion editorials, and even memes. In a world overloaded with noise and narratives, this quiet image still commands attention. It invites not analysis, but wonder.

In our fast-scrolling age, where images flash and vanish, *Girl with a Pearl Earring* remains motionless—and perhaps, that is its greatest triumph. It does not try to tell us what to think. It simply asks us to look, and keep looking.

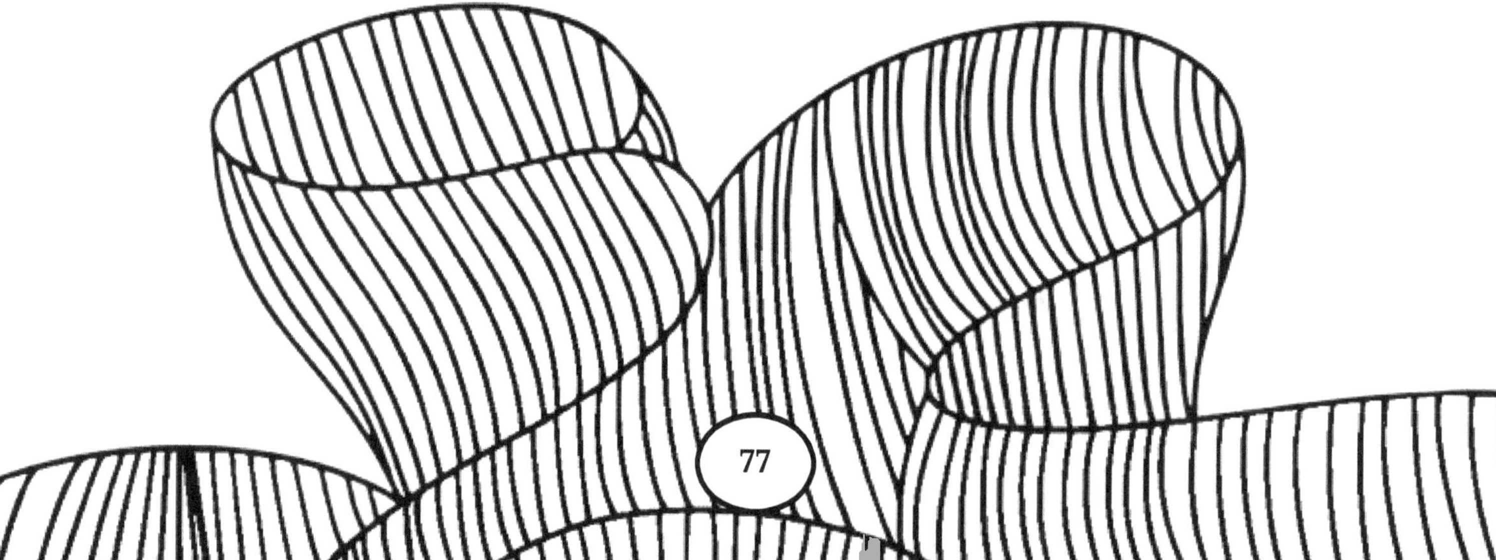

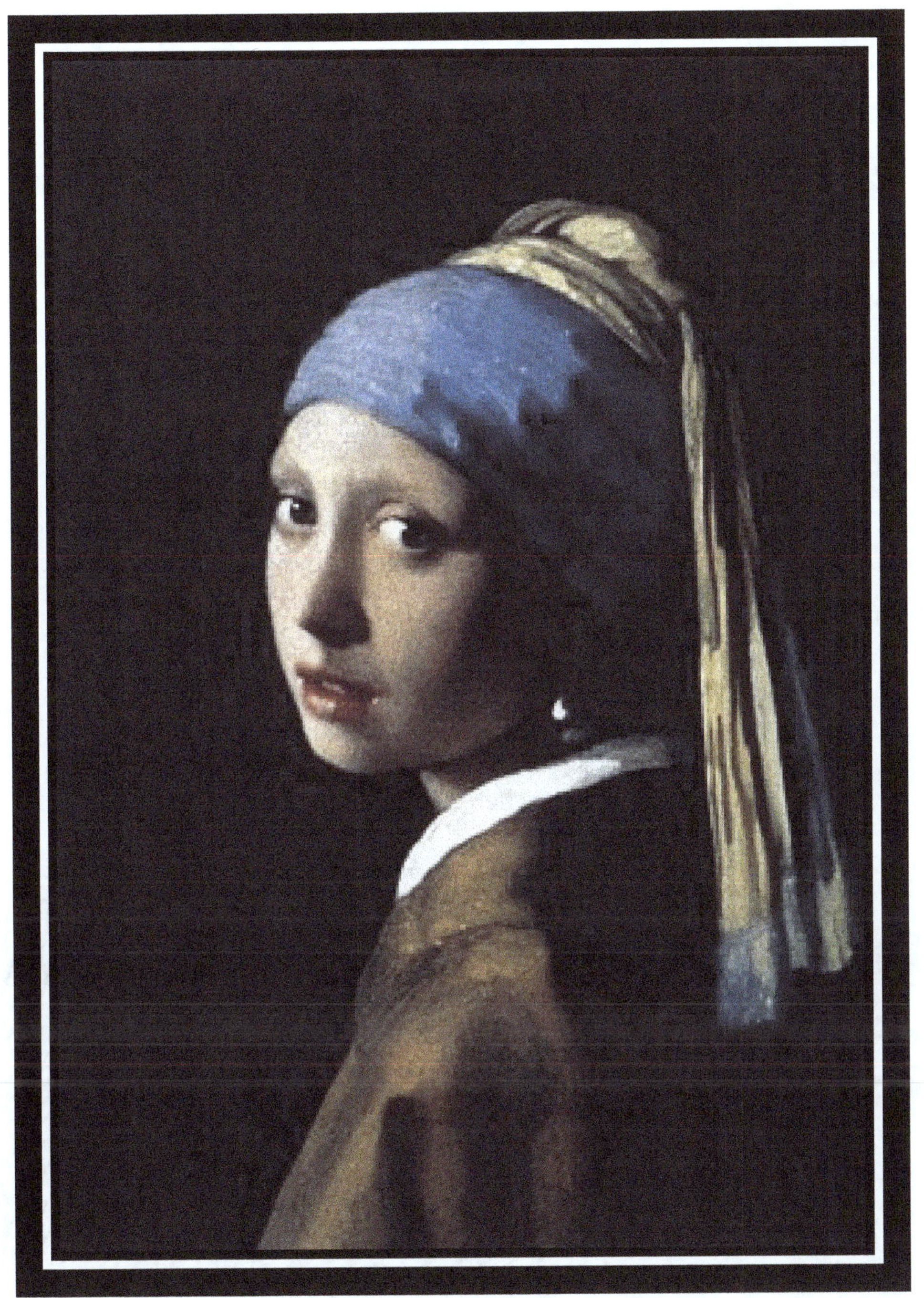

THE GIRL WITH THE PEARL EARRING
(AFTER VERMEER)

She turns in quiet light, a fleeting gaze
A secret held between the dark and dawn.
Her eyes, like shadows, speak in silent ways
While moonlit pearl adorns her ear, withdrawn.

The turban wraps her hair in folds of night
A ribbon bound to stories left untold.
Her face, a canvas bathed in softened light
Holds mysteries the painter's hand controlled.

What dreams reside behind her steady stare –
A hope, a doubt, a future yet unseen?
No words disturb the stillness resting there
A moment caught where time has stood between.

The pearl swings gently, whispering of seas
And keeps her grace suspended like a breeze.

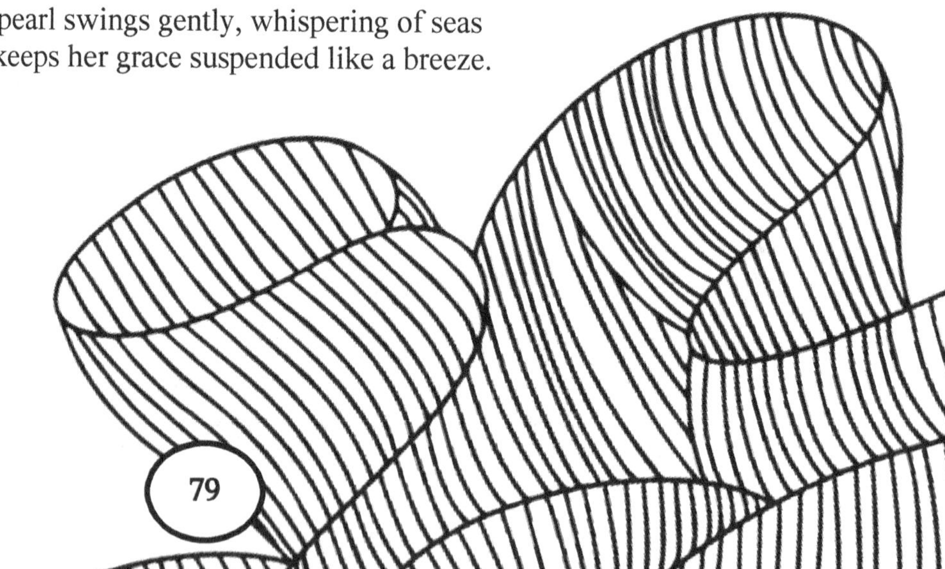

THE GIRL WITH THE PEARL EARRING
(AFTER VERMEER)

In quiet light she turns—a fleeting glance
A moment caught between the dark and dawn.
Her eyes, like shadows deep, invite a world
Unspoken, held in silence and in shade.

The pearl – a drop of moonlight, calm and pure
Suspended at her lobe, a whispered truth.
No words escape, yet stories rise and fall
Within the stillness of her gentle face.

She waits, a secret kept from time's embrace
As if the painter's brush has touched her soul
And frozen breath, a breath that never fades.

The turban wraps in blue her midnight hair
A ribbon tied to histories untold.
Its folds conceal the tides of distant lands
Yet frame the softness of her pale, smooth cheek.

Behind her gaze, the world is turned to paint
A quiet study in the art of light
Where shadows fall like silk upon her skin
And mystery clings to every quiet line.

What thoughts lie hidden in the depths of those eyes?
A flicker caught between defiance, hope

Or wonder born of youth yet unexplored?

She holds the stillness like a sacred vow
A moment caught between becoming and
The past that waits beyond the painter's hand.

No sound intrudes upon this silent pose
No breath disturbs the calm of captured time.
Yet in her gaze a thousand stories dance
Of fleeting glances, longing, and unknown
Adventures written only in the light.

The pearl swings gently, whispering of seas
Of trade and voyages that cross the globe.
A treasure born beneath far distant waves
Now resting close beside a fragile grace

The girl who holds the world within her eyes,
Forever caught between the dark and dawn.

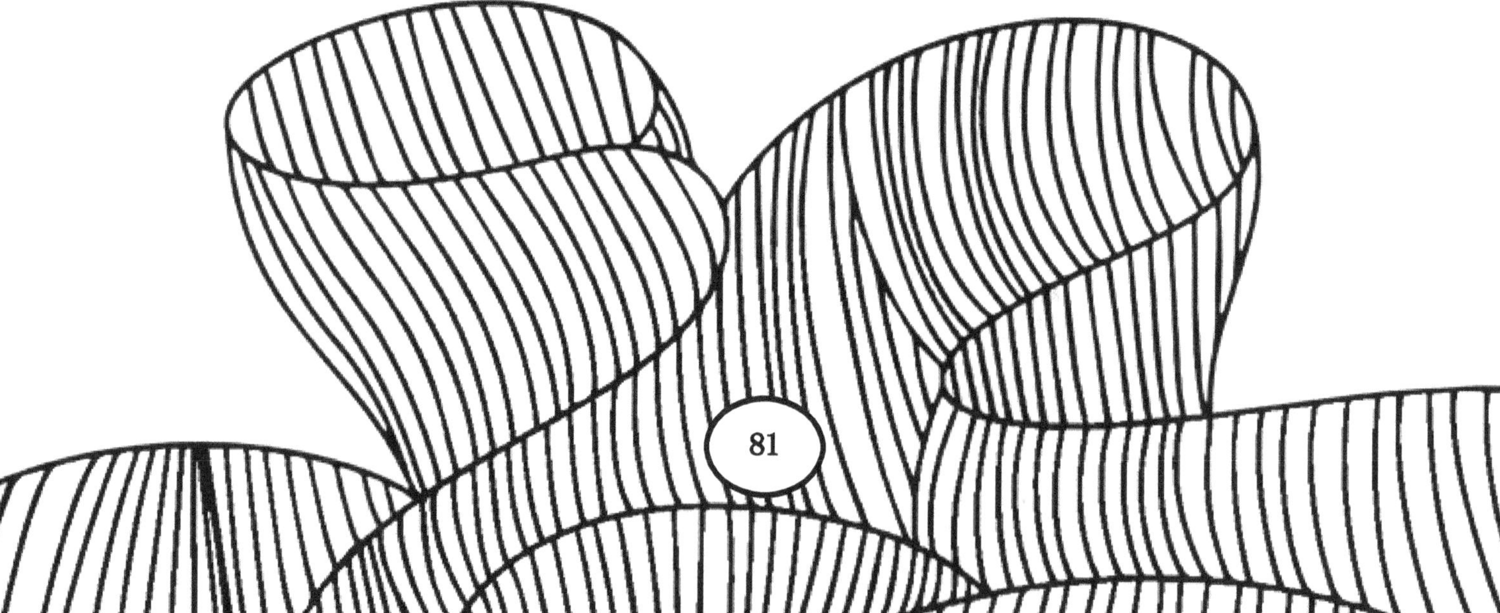

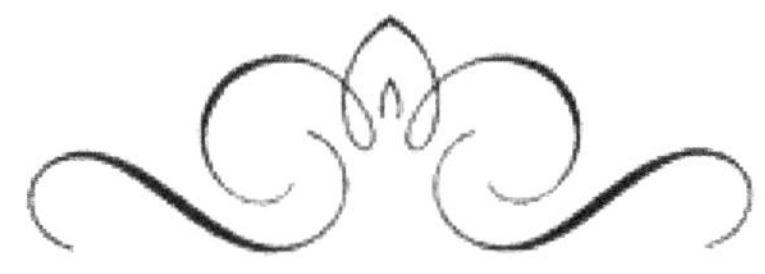

THE KISS BY GUSTAV KLIMT

A GOLDEN EMBRACE OF LOVE

Gustav Klimt's *The Kiss* stands as one of the most renowned images in modern art, a radiant celebration of intimacy, passion, and the ethereal beauty of human connection. Painted between 1907 and 1908, during Klimt's "Golden Phase," this masterpiece transcends mere representation, inviting viewers into a world where love is both sacred and sensuous, wrapped in shimmering gold leaf and intricate patterns.

At first glance, *The Kiss* captivates with its opulent use of gold—an element Klimt incorporated not just as decoration but as a symbol of transcendence and the divine. The couple, locked in a tender embrace, appears almost otherworldly, their forms merging into a luminous tapestry that blends the human with the mystical. This luminous quality elevates the intimate moment beyond the mundane, suggesting that love itself is a form of spiritual illumination.

Klimt's composition is striking in its symmetry and abstraction. The man leans gently over the woman, who kneels in submission, her eyes closed in a state of blissful surrender. Their bodies are adorned with elaborate robes decorated in geometric shapes for the man and delicate floral motifs for the woman. This contrast hints at the interplay of masculine and feminine energies, grounding the passion in a universal harmony.

Unlike traditional portraits of couples, Klimt avoids realism in favour of stylisation, where patterns and colours convey emotional depth more than facial expressions or physical details. The golden background envelops the figures, creating a halo effect that blurs the line between the earthly and the divine. The textured surface—crafted with gold and silver leaf—adds a three-dimensional quality, inviting viewers to feel the tactile richness of the moment.

Beyond its visual splendour, *The Kiss* is a reflection of Klimt's fascination with the human psyche and eroticism. His work emerged during the Vienna Secession, a movement that challenged academic art and embraced modernity, psychology, and symbolism. Through *The Kiss*, Klimt explores not just romantic love but the primal urge for connection and the vulnerability it entails.

The painting's universal appeal lies in its ability to evoke emotions without words. Whether viewed as a symbol of passionate love, spiritual unity, or artistic innovation, *The Kiss* resonates across cultures and generations. It remains a testament to Klimt's genius, who transformed a simple embrace into an eternal dance of light, colour, and emotion.

In an era where art often distances itself from the viewer, *The Kiss* invites us in, reminding us that beneath the surface of patterns and gold lies the timeless human story: the yearning to be seen, touched, and loved.

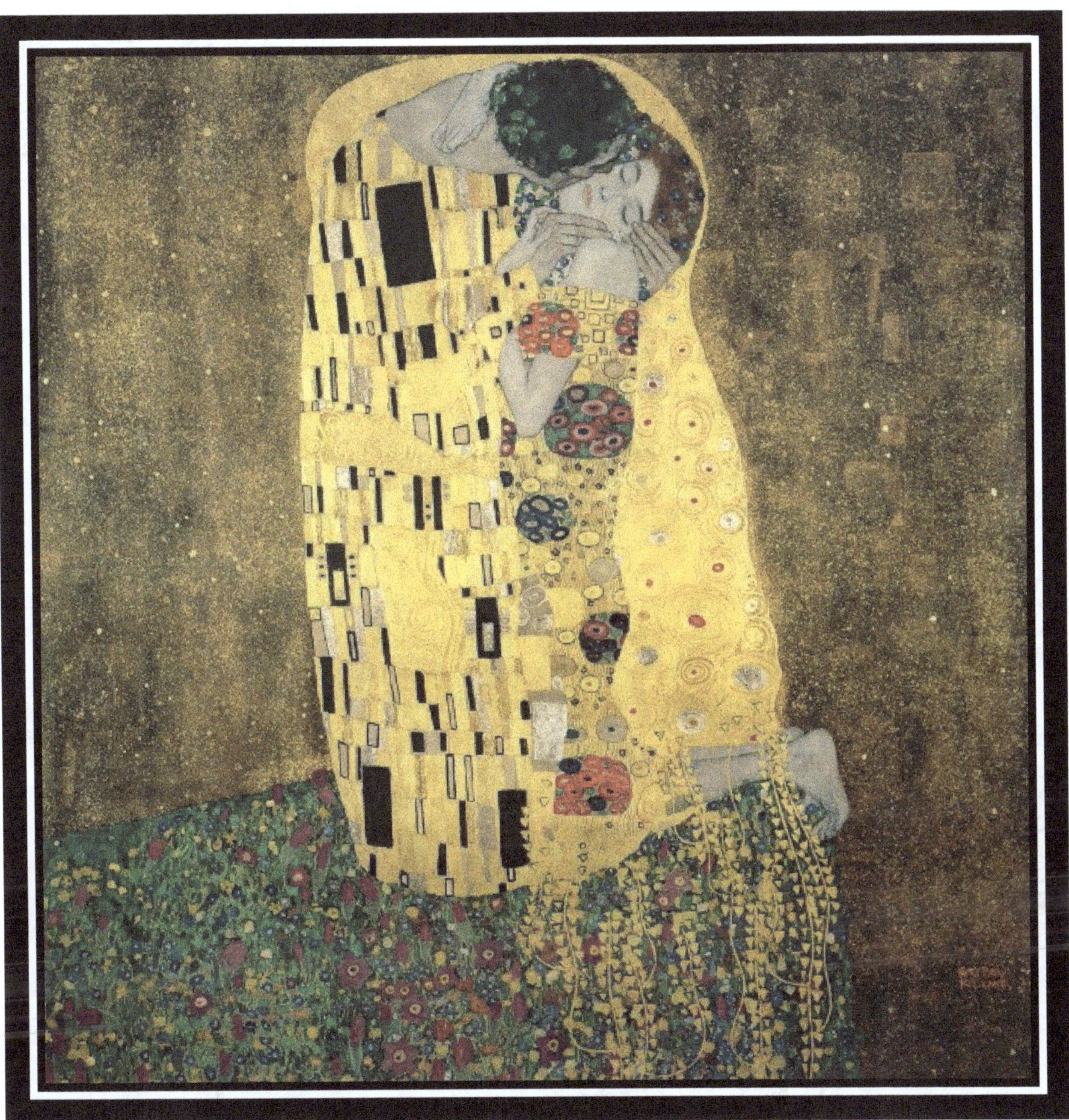

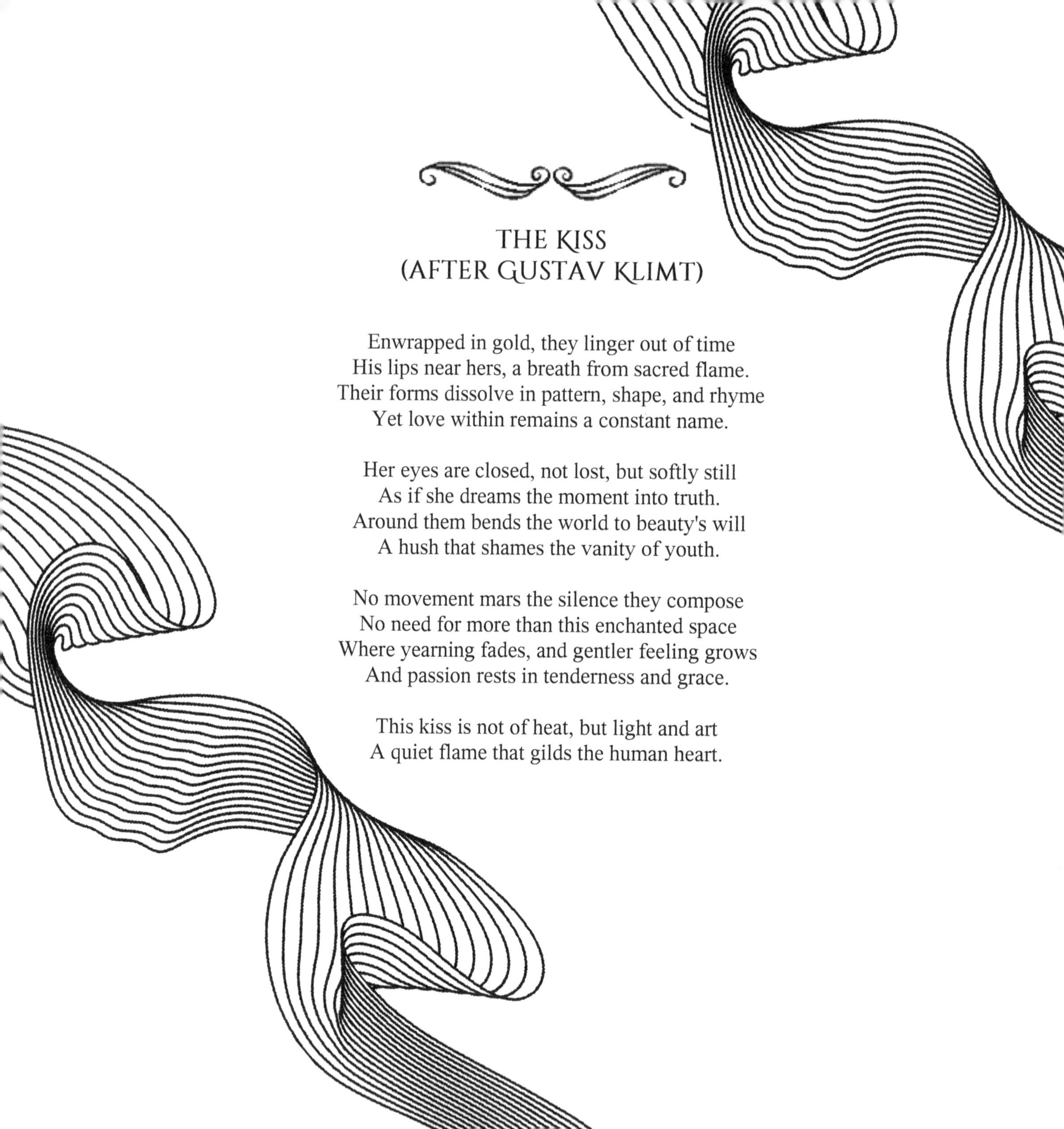

THE KISS
(AFTER GUSTAV KLIMT)

Enwrapped in gold, they linger out of time
His lips near hers, a breath from sacred flame.
Their forms dissolve in pattern, shape, and rhyme
Yet love within remains a constant name.

Her eyes are closed, not lost, but softly still
As if she dreams the moment into truth.
Around them bends the world to beauty's will
A hush that shames the vanity of youth.

No movement mars the silence they compose
No need for more than this enchanted space
Where yearning fades, and gentler feeling grows
And passion rests in tenderness and grace.

This kiss is not of heat, but light and art
A quiet flame that gilds the human heart.

THE KISS
(AFTER GUSTAV KLIMT)

They stand as though the world has slipped away
Wrapped in a hush of gold and flame and sleep.
His face bends low, not hurried, but enthralled
A prayer in flesh, a whisper through the dusk.

No time remains beyond this gilded edge
Where form dissolves to pattern, skin to light
And limbs are draped in tessellated grace
As if love's language is geometry.

Her eyes are shut, not shunning but released
Her mouth a bloom just brushed by breath and time.
The earth beneath is scarcely earth at all
A meadow wrought from silence, dream, and dusk.

Around them swirls a shimmer not of stars
But longing hammered thin, as gold-leaf is
That clings like memory to every fold
And turns desire into a sacred veil.

They do not move, nor need they ever stir
The moment hangs, complete, and cannot break.
Not passion, no, not merely that, but peace
The stillness when the ache has found its end.

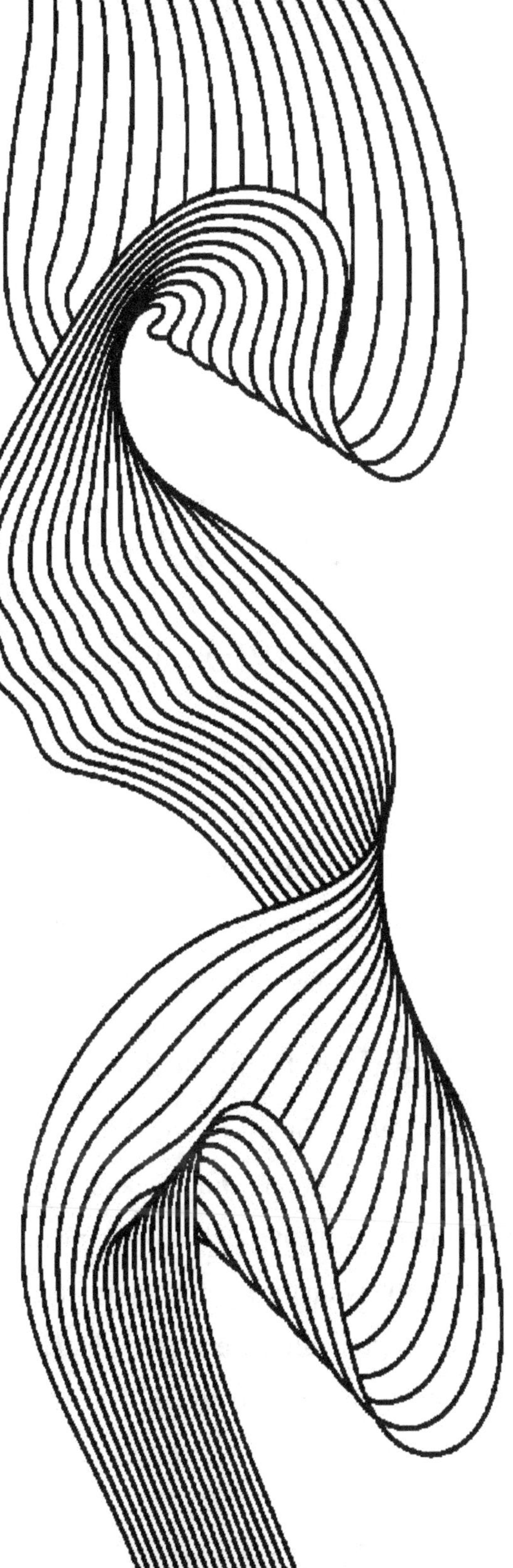

The Liffey Swim
by Jack B. Yeats

A Vivid Celebration of Dublin's Spirit

Jack B. Yeats, one of Ireland's most celebrated painters, masterfully captures the energy, vibrancy, and cultural essence of Dublin in his iconic work *The Liffey Swim*. Far more than a simple depiction of an annual swimming event, this painting pulses with the rhythm of the city and its people, inviting viewers to immerse themselves in a uniquely Irish experience that blends sport, community, and tradition.

A Snapshot of Dublin Life

The Liffey Swim, an open-water race held annually in the River Liffey, has long been a beloved Dublin tradition dating back to 1920. Yeats, renowned for his ability to animate Irish scenes with emotional depth and expressive brushwork, channels this cultural pulse in his painting. Instead of focusing solely on the swimmers or the race itself, he broadens the scene to encompass the entire atmosphere surrounding the event—the cheering crowd, the muddy riverbanks, and the weather-worn buildings lining the river, all rendered with a raw, almost frenetic energy.

STYLE AND TECHNIQUE – A DANCE OF COLOUR AND MOVEMENT

Yeats's distinctive style in *The Liffey Swim* breaks away from conventional realism, opting instead for a dynamic interplay of colour, form, and texture. His brushstrokes swirl and collide, mimicking the choppy waters of the Liffey and the chaotic excitement of the race. The painting's palette is rich yet earthy, with deep blues and greens contrasting sharply against bursts of fiery oranges and reds that evoke the fervour of the crowd and the human spirit.

The composition itself is lively and somewhat fragmented, echoing the movement of the swimmers slicing through water. Figures merge and blur, suggesting both individual struggle and collective celebration, a testament to Yeats's ability to capture human emotion and social interaction in a single frame.

SYMBOLISM AND CULTURAL RESONANCE

Beneath the surface of this energetic portrayal lies a deeper narrative about Dublin's resilience and community cohesion. *The Liffey Swim*, as depicted by Yeats, symbolises more than just an athletic contest; it stands as a metaphor for life's challenges and the enduring spirit of those who face them. The swimmers pushing through the cold, turbulent river become a vivid emblem of persistence and camaraderie.

Moreover, the painting reflects the socio-political climate of Ireland during Yeats's lifetime—a period marked by upheaval, identity formation, and a burgeoning sense of national pride. By capturing an event rooted in local tradition, Yeats celebrates Dublin's unique cultural identity and the everyday heroism of its citizens.

LEGACY OF THE LIFFEY SWIM IN IRISH ART

The Liffey Swim remains a touchstone in Irish art for its vibrant portrayal of city life and its powerful evocation of communal spirit. Jack B. Yeats's work transcends mere representation to become a living document of Dublin's heart and soul. Through this painting, viewers gain a glimpse of a moment frozen in time but teeming with life—a snapshot of a city that thrives on its people's grit, passion, and connection to one another.

The Liffey Swim is not just a painting about a race; it is a celebration of Dublin's pulse, an ode to human endurance, and a testament to Jack B. Yeats's unparalleled ability to capture the essence of Irish culture on canvas.

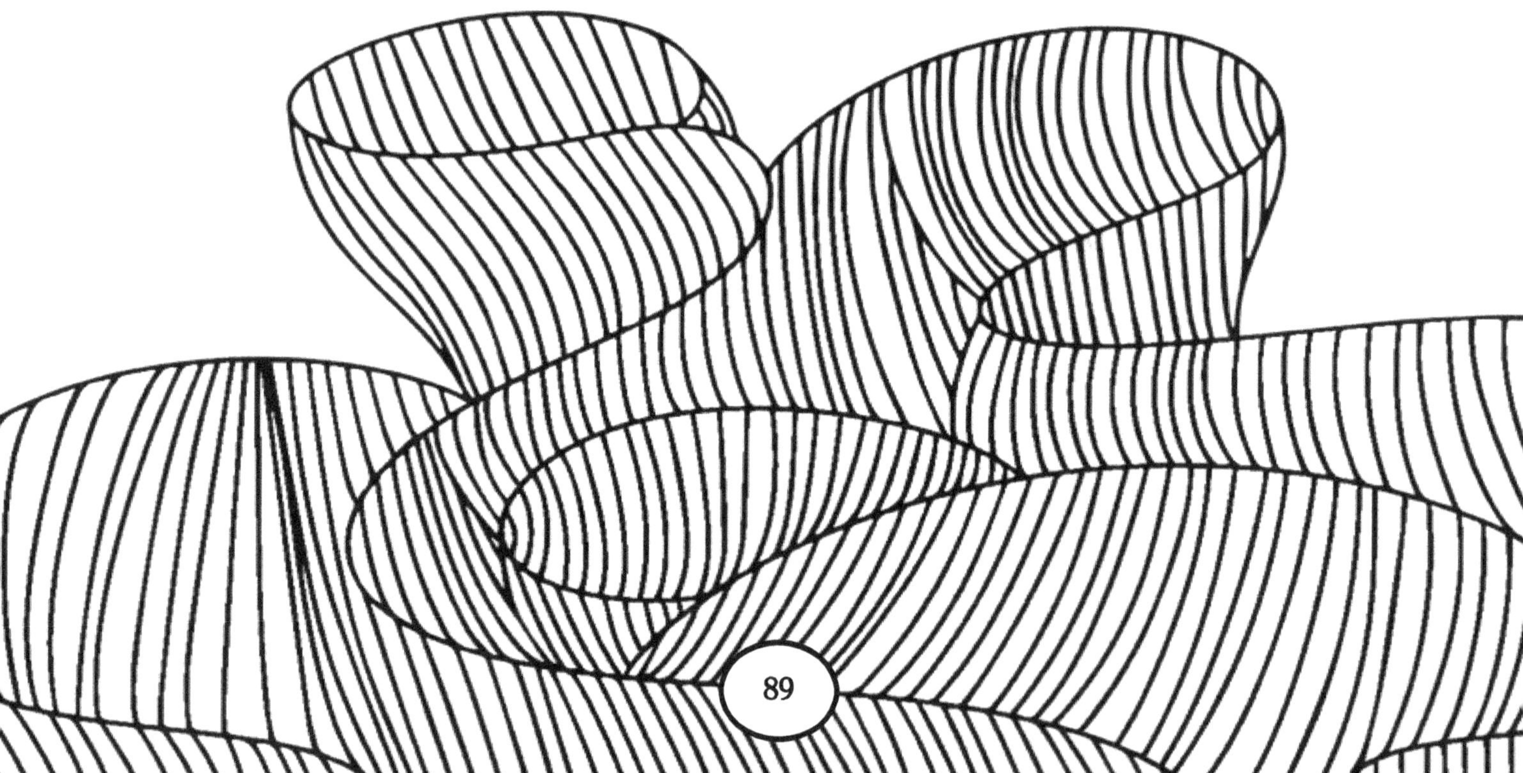

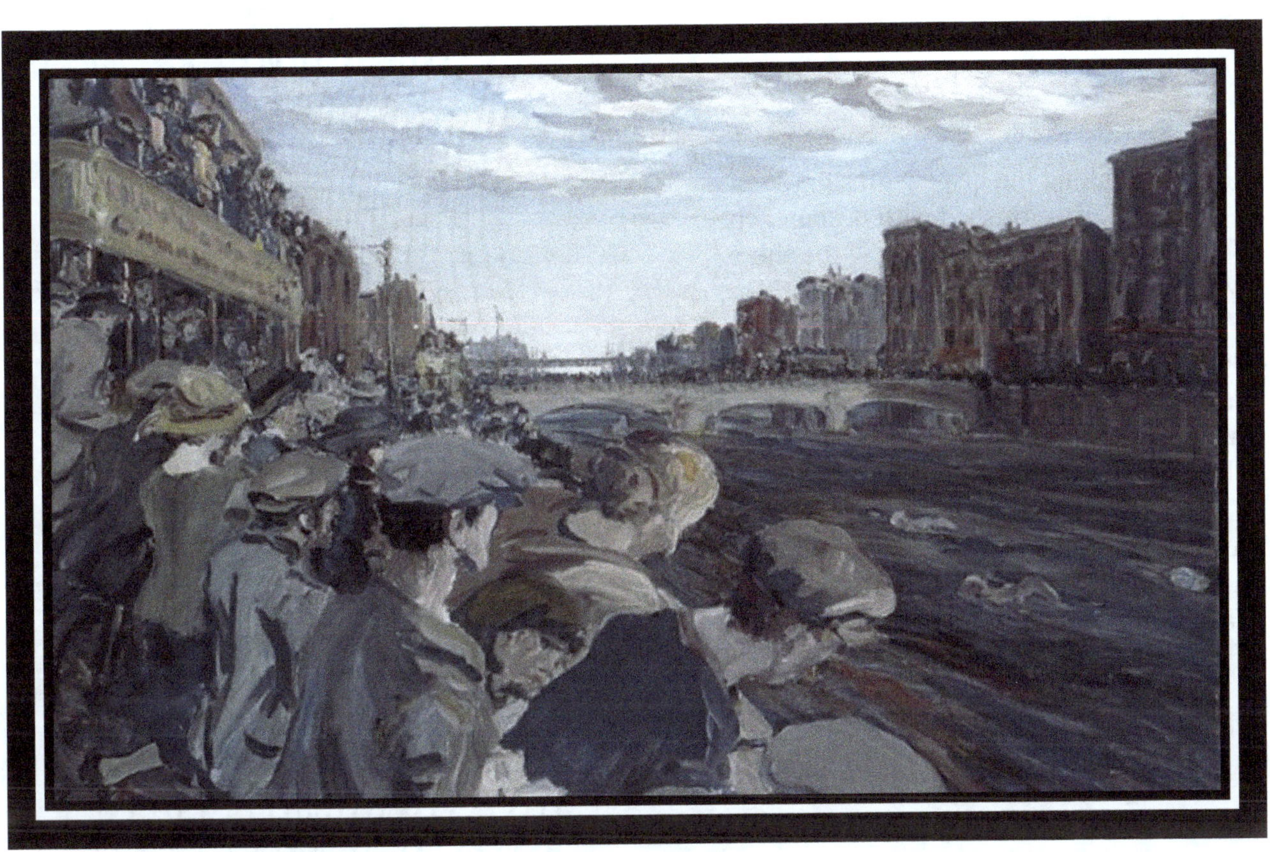

THE LIFFEY SWIM
(AFTER JACK B. YEATS, 1923)

The crowd along the quay begins to roar
A thousand faces flushed with heat and cheer
They press in close, a wall along the shore
While swimmers cut the river without fear.

Beneath the summer sky, the Liffey churns
Its muddy heart alive with stroke and shout
While Yeats, with steady hand and gaze, discerns
The soul the city silently casts out.

A banner flares, a boy climbs high to see
An old one prays, a lad begins to bet
Each figure caught in bright eternity
Though time may turn, they will not fade or set.

Through paint and crowd and water's restless hymn
We see the heart of Dublin in a swim.

THE LIFFEY SWIM
(AFTER JACK B. YEATS)

Along the quays the shouting gathers force
A tide of faces, flushed with joy and cheer
Crowd tight as bricks along the Liffey's edge.
Their cries are flung like gulls above the stream
Where swimmers churn, defying city tides.

Paint, thick and fevered, brings the scene to life
Not still, but surging, laced with Dublin's pulse
A swirl of blue, of red, of skin and pride
The bathers stroke through muddy, brackish hope
While banners wave like tongues of restless flame.

The painter stands apart, yet not alone
His brush a keel to navigate the noise
He knows this crowd, its dreams, its griefs, its jests
Knows how the Liffey holds them, like a breath
Too long inside the chest before it breaks.

Each figure leans into its own small myth
The paper boy who climbs a cart to see
The shawled old woman clutching rosary
The lads with caps askew, who bet on names
They'll never meet but shout for all the same.

And underneath, the water bears them all
The racers, yes, but also time and place

The gathered city mirrored in a swim
Half ritual, half reckless summer dare
Half prayer to something riverine and vast.

Yeats paints not merely what the moment shows
But what it means – this tangle of the now
And what persists when all the crowds have gone
The Liffey keeps its secrets in its silt
But every stroke disturbs the past to light.

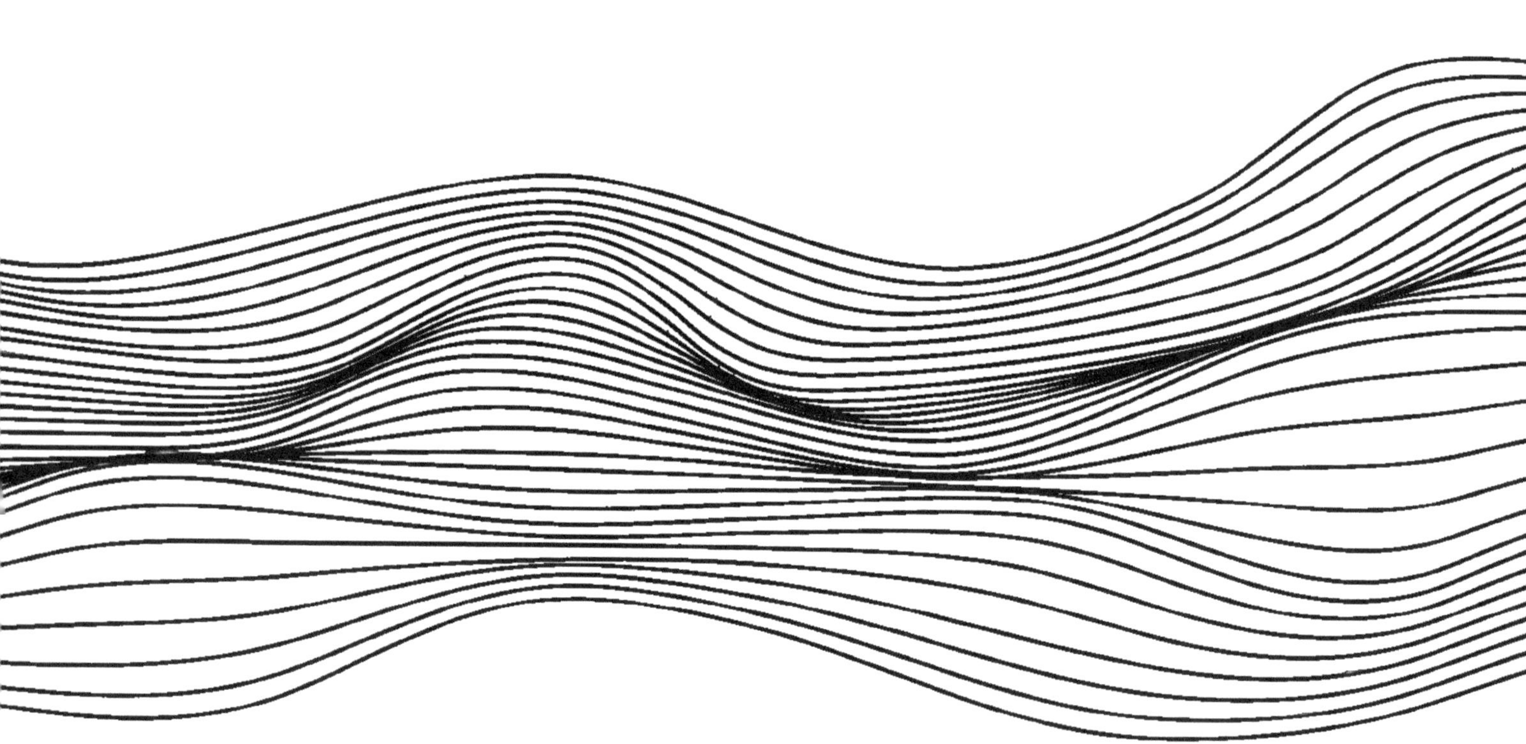

THE ENIGMATIC SMILE

UNVEILING THE MYSTERY OF LEONARDO DA VINCI'S MONA LISA

Few artworks have captivated the world like Leonardo da Vinci's *Mona Lisa*. Painted in the early 16th century during the Italian Renaissance, this portrait has transcended mere artistry to become a cultural icon shrouded in mystery, speculation, and admiration. But what makes the *Mona Lisa* so unique, and why does it continue to fascinate audiences five centuries later?

A PORTRAIT LIKE NO OTHER

At first glance, the *Mona Lisa* may seem like a simple portrait of a woman seated against a dreamlike landscape. Yet, it is precisely this apparent simplicity that conceals its profound complexity. Painted between 1503 and 1506, with possible touches added later, Leonardo employed a technique called *sfumato*, which involves the delicate blending of colours and tones to create a soft, almost smoky transition between light and shadow. This technique breathes life into the figure, allowing her to seem both solid and ethereal at once.

THE WOMAN BEHIND THE SMILE

Who exactly is the *Mona Lisa*? Most art historians agree she is Lisa Gherardini, the wife of a wealthy Florentine merchant. Yet, da Vinci's portrayal transcends mere likeness. The woman's expression—famous for its ambiguity—fluctuates depending on the viewer's angle and focus. Her smile is neither fully joyous nor sombre, creating an elusive emotional resonance that has sparked endless interpretations. Is she amused? Secretive? Melancholic? The smile invites us into a silent dialogue with her soul.

A LANDSCAPE OF SYMBOLISM

Behind her, the landscape unfolds in a surreal, almost otherworldly panorama of winding paths, serene waters, and rugged mountains. Some scholars suggest this backdrop symbolises the harmony between humanity and nature, a reflection of Renaissance ideals. Others believe the mysterious setting hints at a journey—both physical and spiritual—inviting viewers to explore the realms beyond the immediate.

THE ARTISTRY OF INNOVATION

Leonardo was not only a master painter but also a scientist and inventor. His keen understanding of anatomy, light, and perspective shines through in the *Mona Lisa*. The subtle asymmetry of her face, the intricate detailing of her hands, and the delicate interplay of light across her features demonstrates a revolutionary approach to portraiture that broke away from the flat, rigid representations common at the time.

THE LEGACY AND MYSTIQUE

The *Mona Lisa*'s story didn't end with its creation. Over the centuries, it has survived theft, vandalism, and countless restorations. Its theft from the Louvre in 1911 by an Italian nationalist only fuelled its fame, transforming the painting into a symbol of national pride and universal mystery. Today, it stands behind bulletproof glass in Paris, watched over by millions who flock to catch a glimpse of the elusive smile.

WHY THE MONA LISA MATTERS TODAY

In a world saturated with images and instant gratification, the *Mona Lisa* reminds us of the power of subtlety and patience. It teaches that beauty is not always loud or obvious; sometimes, it is hidden in the quiet interplay of light, shadow, and expression. Leonardo's masterpiece invites endless curiosity and reflection—an eternal puzzle that challenges us to look deeper, to wonder more, and to appreciate the artistry of human expression.

The *Mona Lisa* is more than a painting; it is a timeless conversation between artist, subject, and viewer—a delicate dance of mystery and mastery that continues to inspire and intrigue the world.

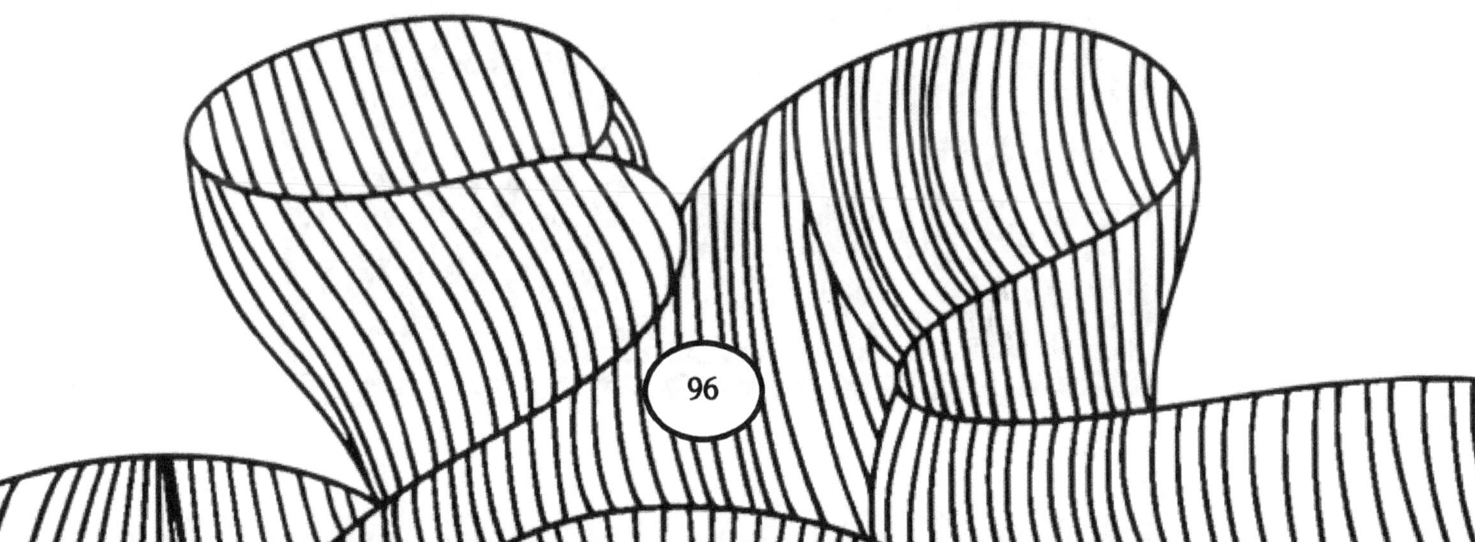

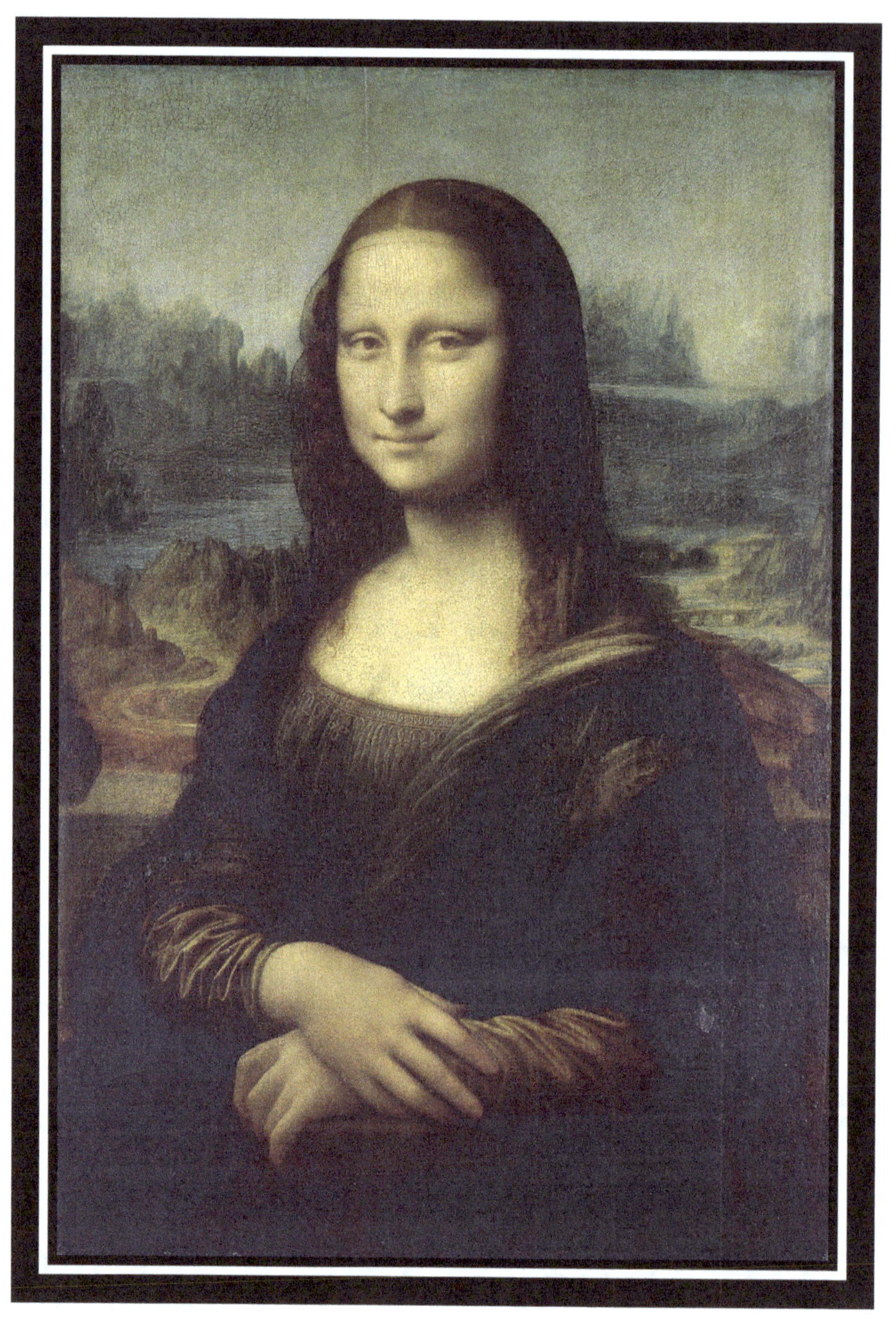

THE SMILE OF LISA
(AFTER LEONARDO DA VINCI)

She holds a silence deeper than the frame
A gaze that floats beyond the glass and wall.
Though centuries have passed, she's still the same—
Serene, untouched, and never one to fall.
Her smile, half-formed, is neither joy nor jest
But some soft thought the lips dare not reveal.
No gem adorns her brow, no need for dress
For all her power lies in what we feel.

Behind her rise the roads of dream and stone
Where nature twists in shapes not fully known.
She watches us, and yet she is alone
A world within herself, a self, full-grown.
What truth she keeps, no eye or art can steal
The soul of silence taught the brush to feel.

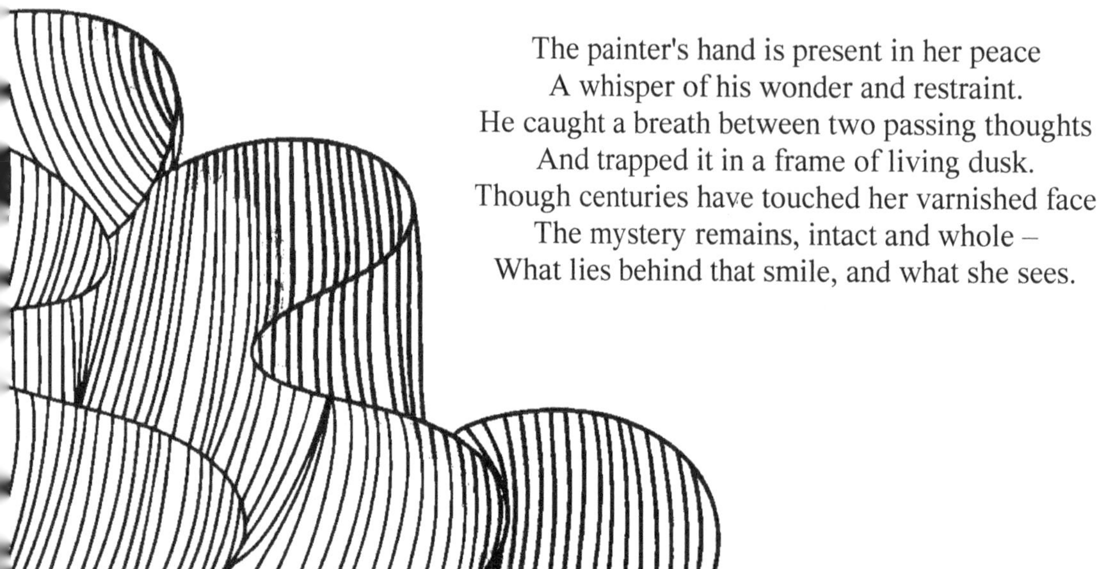

THE MONA LISA
(AFTER LEONARDO DA VINCI)

She sits in silence, gazing out through time
A smile that hovers just beyond the grasp
As if she knows the question yet unasked
And guards the answer in a hush of oil.
Her eyes, twin pools of shadow, seem to shift
Not fixed on us, but looking through the world
As though her sight belonged to something else.

No jewel adorns her brow – no gilded thread
Distracts the viewer from her steady poise.
She is composed of stillness and of doubt
A balance drawn between the real and dream.
Behind her, hills and winding roads recede
As if the world grew stranger as it stretched
Becoming myth the further back it goes.

The painter's hand is present in her peace
A whisper of his wonder and restraint.
He caught a breath between two passing thoughts
And trapped it in a frame of living dusk.
Though centuries have touched her varnished face
The mystery remains, intact and whole –
What lies behind that smile, and what she sees.

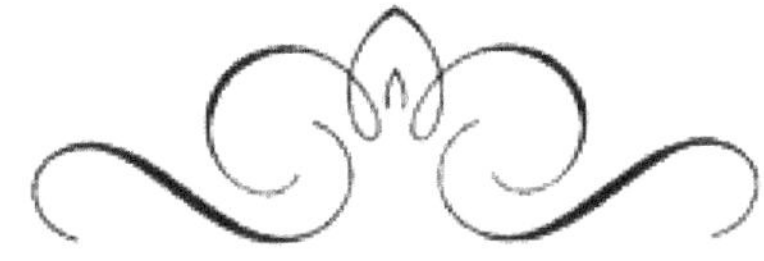

THE PERSISTENCE OF MEMORY

SALVADOR DALÍ'S DREAMSCAPE OF TIME

In the vast realm of surrealism, Salvador Dalí's *The Persistence of Memory* stands as a timeless beacon—a painting that twists reality and perception into a dreamlike tableau. Created in 1931, this iconic work continues to captivate viewers with its enigmatic imagery and profound meditation on the nature of time.

At first glance, *The Persistence of Memory* presents a strange, almost barren landscape under a calm blue sky. Yet the viewer's eye is immediately drawn to the melting clocks draped over various objects—an unsettling distortion that challenges the rigid, mechanical precision we associate with time. These clocks, soft and fluid, seem to defy the fundamental laws of physics, embodying Dalí's fascination with the elastic, subjective experience of time rather than its objective measurement.

Dalí's inspiration for this imagery reportedly came from a surrealist moment triggered by the sight of Camembert cheese melting in the sun. This simple, everyday observation transformed into a powerful visual metaphor: time itself melts away, bends, and warps under the pressures of memory, dreams, and consciousness.

The painting's dreamscape is populated with strange objects—a distorted face, perhaps a self-portrait of Dalí himself, lying limp and abstracted in the centre; ants swarming over a clock, symbolising decay and impermanence; and a distant seashore that anchors the composition in reality. These elements work together to evoke a haunting atmosphere, where time is not linear but fragmented, fluid, and elusive.

More than just a surrealist curiosity, *The Persistence of Memory* invites reflection on the human experience of time. It suggests that time, far from being a fixed, universal constant, is mutable and subjective, shaped by our memories and emotions. This philosophical undertone resonates deeply, reminding us that our perception of moments can stretch and contract, often slipping away or lingering in unexpected ways.

Dalí's masterful technique—sharp, precise details rendered in a soft, almost hypnotic light—enhances the painting's surreal effect. The contrast between the hyper-realistic texture of the landscape and the dreamlike distortion of the clocks creates a tension that pulls the viewer into a liminal space between reality and fantasy.

Today, *The Persistence of Memory* remains a profound symbol of surrealism and a testament to Dalí's genius in visualising the intangible. It challenges us to reconsider our relationship with time—not as a relentless ticking clock, but as a fluid, persistent memory etched into the canvas of our minds.

In essence, Dalí's masterpiece is not just a painting; it is an invitation to dream, to question, and to embrace the mysterious persistence of memory itself.

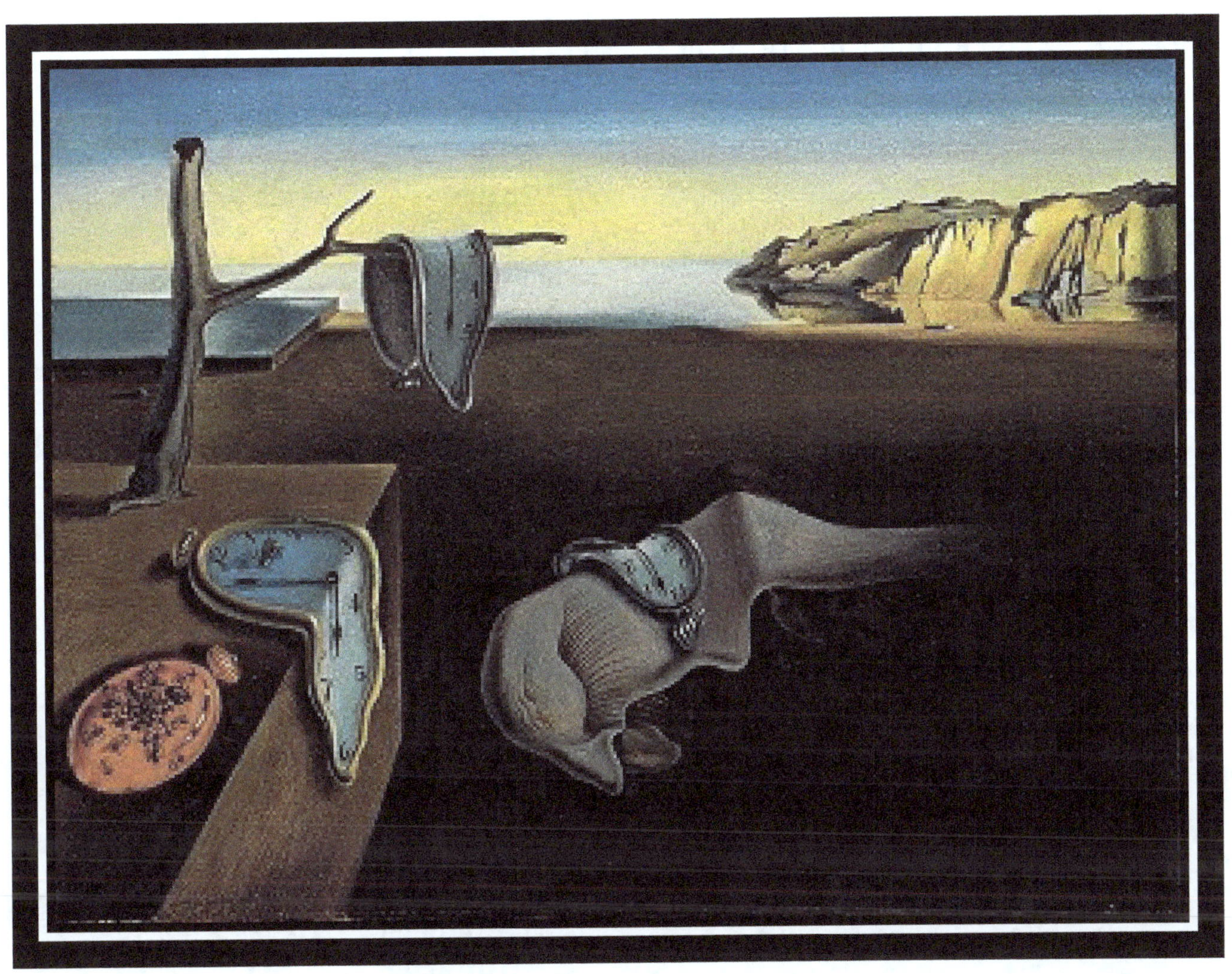

THE PERSISTENCE OF MEMORY
(AFTER SALVADOR DALÍ)

Beneath a sun that burns with distant light
Soft watches drip like wax in endless dream.
The barren cliffs observe the fading sight
Where ants consume the fragile edges' gleam.

Time folds and bends, a shapeless, drifting stream
No rigid pulse to bind the moments tight.
A slumbering face lost in a silent scheme
Between the stone and softness fades from sight.

The sky is stretched in melancholy hue
Where past and present merge and intertwine.
The clocks dissolve, yet memories hold true
In warped embrace beyond the reach of time.

This dream endures a strange and quiet plea
That time is fluid, boundless mystery.

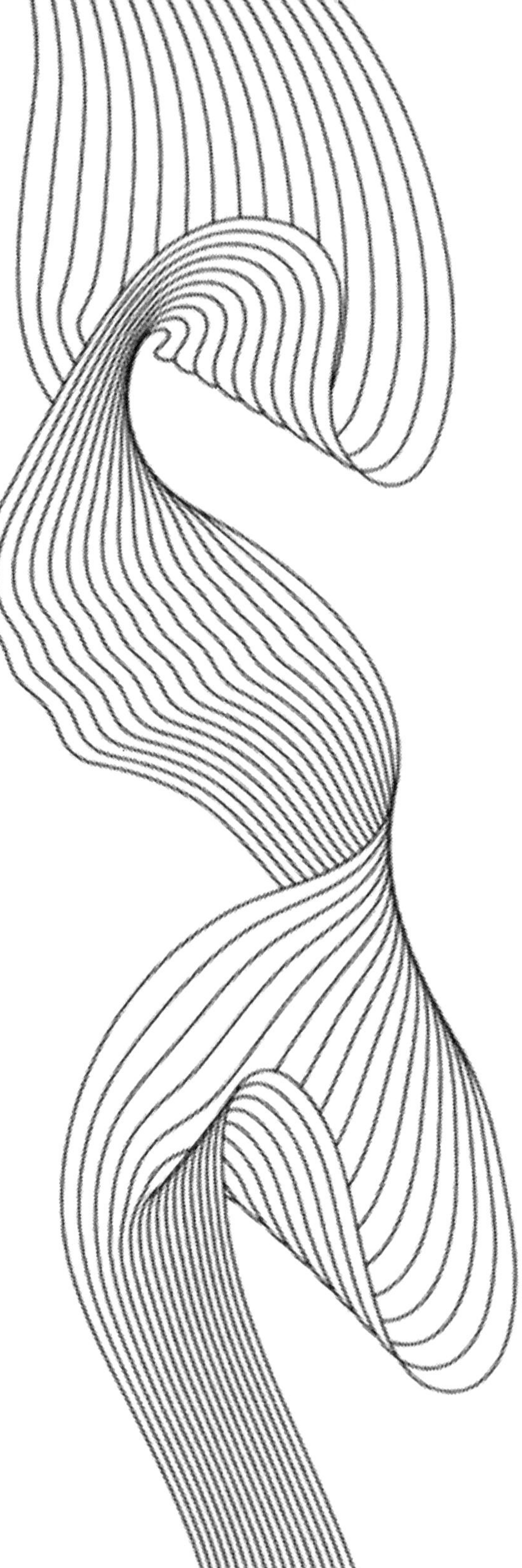

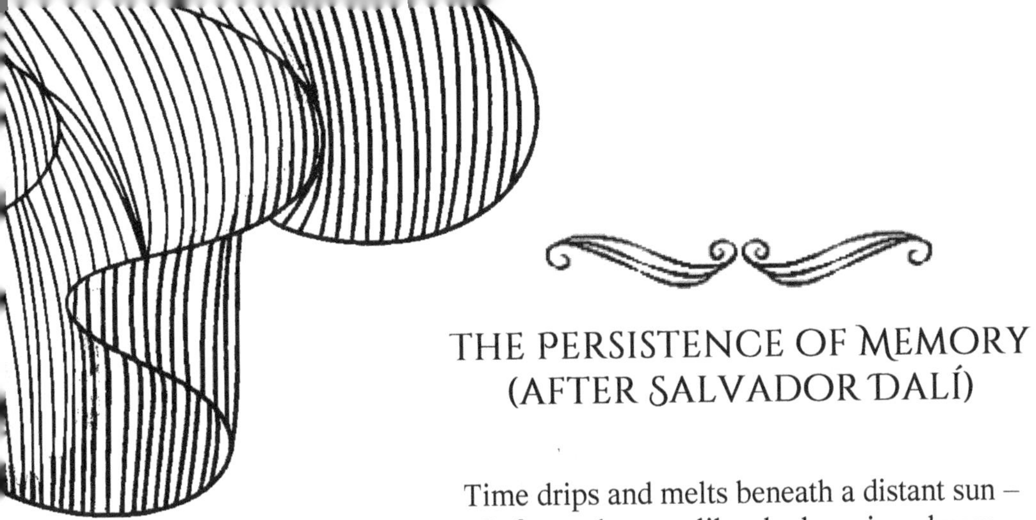

THE PERSISTENCE OF MEMORY
(AFTER SALVADOR DALÍ)

Time drips and melts beneath a distant sun –
Soft watches sag like shadows in a dream.
A barren landscape stretches far and still
Where ants consume the remnants of the mind.
The cliffs stand silent, watching moments fade
While clocks distort the pulse of what we know.
Surreal and fragile, memory decays
Yet lingers stubborn in the empty air.

Between the folds of softness and the stone
Reality and fantasy entwine
Unfolding truths that reason cannot hold.
A twisted face lies sleeping on the ground
Its lashes thick with time's relentless weight
As if the mind itself has slipped away
Abandoned in the haze of shifting shapes.

The sky bends low, a melancholy blue –
Reflecting depths of thought that have no shore.
Each hour bends, refusing strict confines
Eluding grasp like smoke that slips through hands.
Here time is fluid, never strict or fixed
A paradox within the waking world.

The melting clocks, like drips of wax, defy
The order that the human heart demands.

They tell a tale beyond the ticking sound
Where past and present fold and intertwine.
Persistence lies not in the ticking beat
But in the strange endurance of the mind.

And so the dream endures, a frozen flow
A silent song that only time can hear.
The Persistence of Memory remains
A whispered secret carved in endless light.

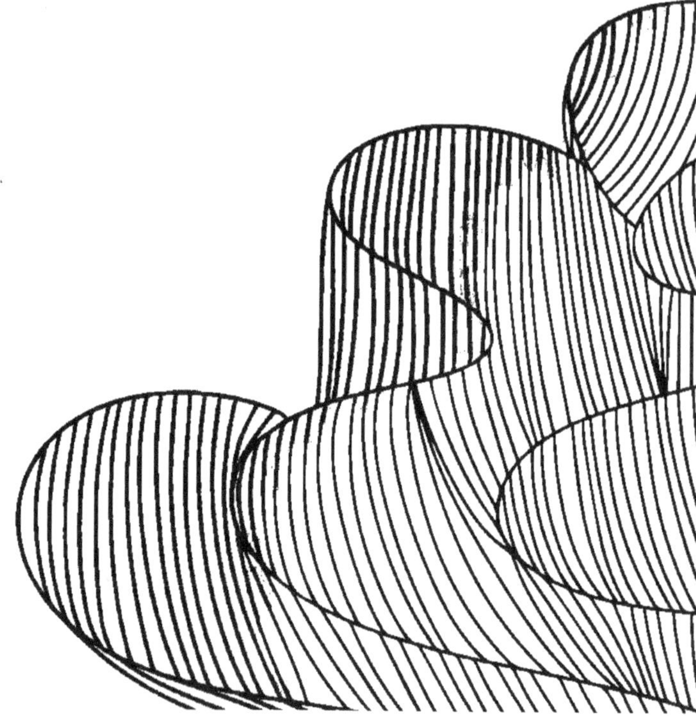

THE SCREAM BY EDVARD MUNCH

A HAUNTING ECHO OF MODERN ANXIETY

Edvard Munch's *The Scream* stands as one of the most famed and unsettling images in the history of art. Far beyond a mere painting, it is a vivid visual scream into the void—a raw, emotional outcry that captures the profound anxieties of the human experience. Painted in 1893, this work transcends time and culture, becoming a universal symbol of existential dread.

MORE THAN JUST A PAINTING – A PSYCHOLOGICAL PORTRAIT

At first glance, *The Scream* depicts a ghostly figure clutching its face, mouth open in a silent cry against a swirling, tumultuous backdrop. But to reduce it to a snapshot of horror or fear misses its deeper resonance. Edvard Munch was grappling with the inner turmoil of modern life—alienation, despair, and the relentless pressure of an increasingly chaotic world. The figure's distorted form and the landscape's feverish colours work together to convey a moment of overwhelming psychological crisis.

THE INSPIRATION BEHIND THE VISION

Munch himself described the inspiration in a diary entry, recounting a walk at sunset when he suddenly felt "a great, infinite scream pass through nature." This wasn't a scream heard aloud but a sensation of the world itself crying out in anguish. That sensation became the beating heart of the painting, a visualisation of the intangible feeling of panic and isolation.

ARTISTIC TECHNIQUES AND SYMBOLISM

The swirling sky, painted with bold strokes of fiery reds and oranges, suggests a landscape ablaze, reflecting the turmoil within. The undulating lines and unnatural hues reject realism, plunging the viewer into an emotional rather than literal reality. The anguished figure, almost skeletal in appearance, embodies vulnerability and the fragility of the human psyche. The bridge on which the figure stands acts as a liminal space—between safety and chaos, reality and nightmare.

THE IMPACT ON CULTURE AND ART

The Scream has inspired countless reinterpretations, parodies, and homages. Its post expressionistic style has influenced artists who sought to depict emotion over form. Beyond art, it has permeated popular culture, becoming shorthand for fear and anxiety in everything from movies to memes.

WHY THE SCREAM STILL RESONATES

In today's fast-paced, unpredictable world, the raw emotion captured by Munch remains startlingly relevant. It speaks to anyone who has ever felt overwhelmed by invisible pressures or caught in a moment of existential crisis. *The Scream* reminds us that these feelings, though isolating, are shared threads in the fabric of human experience.

Edvard Munch's *The Scream* endures not just as an artwork but as a mirror reflecting the complexities of the human soul—a timeless emblem of fear, vulnerability, and the haunting beauty of emotional truth.

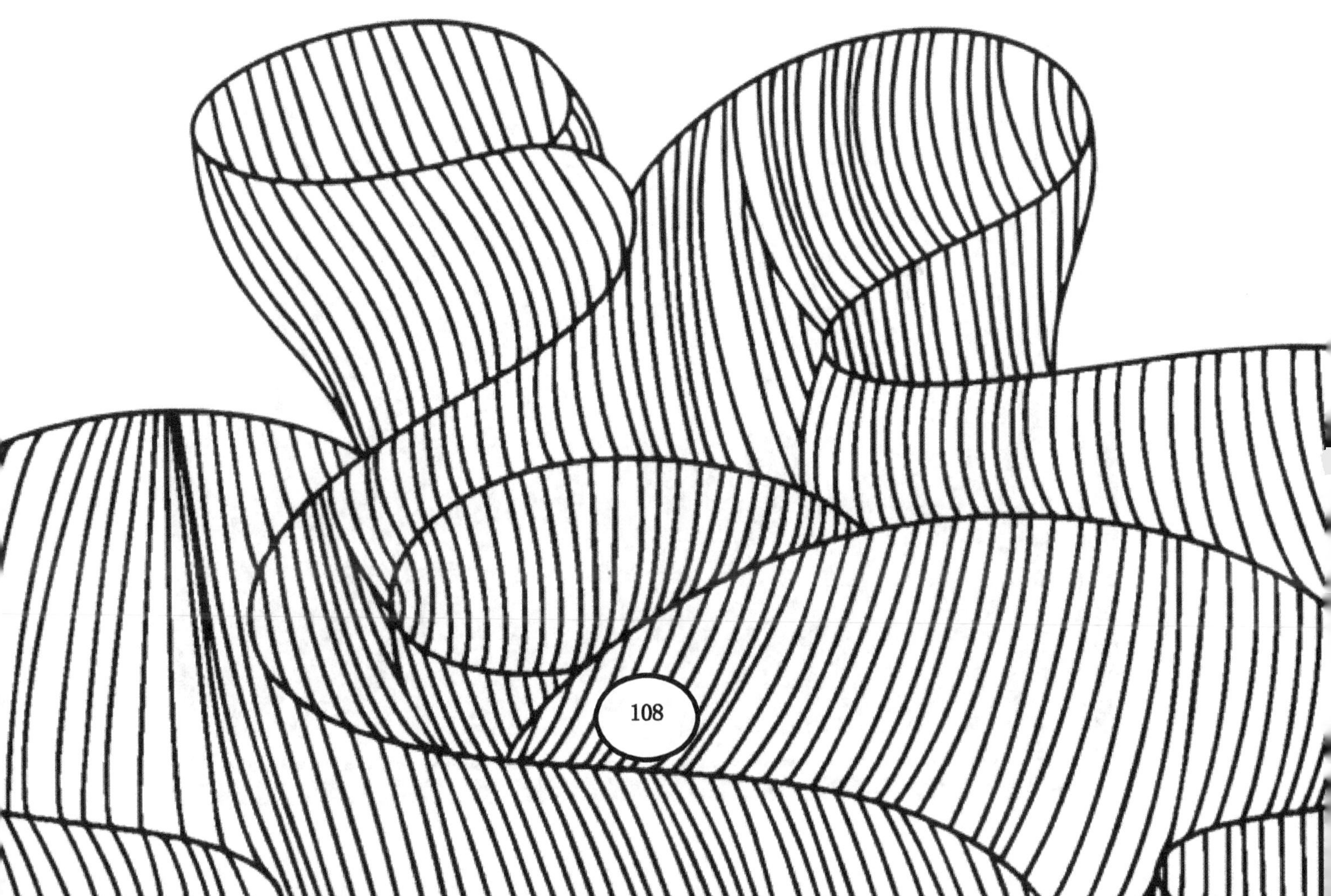

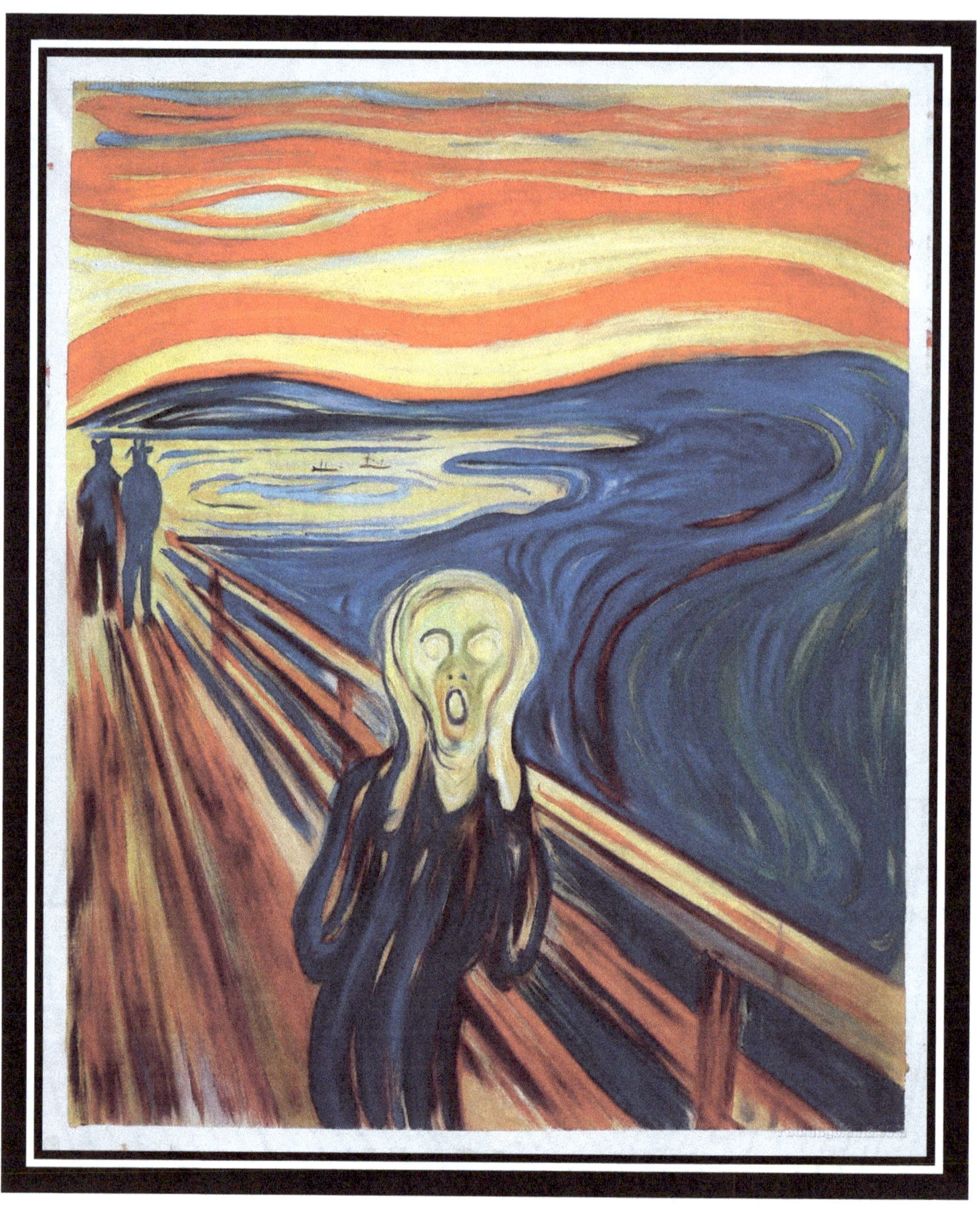

THE SCREAM
(AFTER EDVARD MUNCH)

I walked beneath a sky of burning red
The twilight bent with strange, unsettling weight.
The stillness of the fjord stirred fear and dread
As though the world were held in hands of fate.

Two figures passed, untouched by what I knew
A rising cry that bloomed within my chest.
The colours screamed, the sky turned ghastly hue
And none but I could hear the world's unrest.

My hands rose up to hold my hollow face
While silence throbbed beneath the painted glare.
The bridge became a thin and fragile place
Where self and sky dissolved into the air.

What voice was mine, and what belonged to air?
The scream was all – and I was barely there.

THE SCREAM
(AFTER EDVARD MUNCH)

I walked alone beneath a blood-red sky
The fjord lay still, yet trembled in my mind.
A bridge of wood beneath my hurried steps
Stretched like a thread across the world's despair.
Two figures passed behind, adrift in peace
Unmoved by how the heavens bent and broke.

The air itself grew heavy, sharp, and loud
A shriek of colour clawed across the dusk
And all the world dissolved into that sound.
My hands flew up to cage the cry within
But it had left me – rushing from my bones
A voiceless wail that echoed through the void.

What was it that had torn the veil of dusk
The self unravelling in fear's eclipse?
Or just the soul, laid bare, beneath the sky –
Too small to hold the weight of all that is?
I stood and stared into the endless wave
And knew the scream would never quite be still.

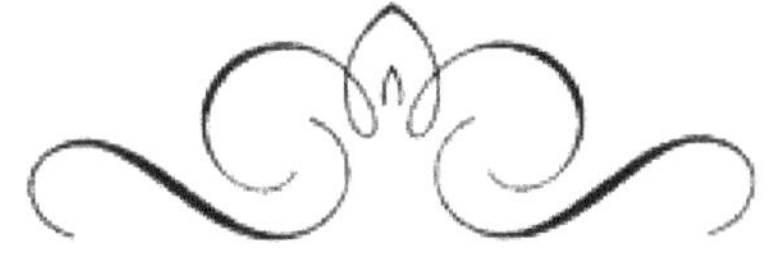

The Sunshade by William Leech

A Quiet Triumph of Light and Leisure

In the landscape of early 20th-century British art, where industrial grit and pastoral nostalgia often collided, *The Sunshade* by William Leech emerges as a luminous oasis. Painted in 1913, this canvas is more than just a depiction of a serene summer afternoon—it's a celebration of light itself, filtered through a master's sensibility for colour, atmosphere, and emotional resonance.

A Scene Bathed in Light

The Sunshade captures a quiet moment: a woman, seated in a sunlit garden, her face softly obscured by the parasol she holds. The composition is simple, yet the painting pulses with vibrancy. Leech's palette is rich with creamy whites, lemon yellows, and softened greens that suggest warmth without aggression. The parasol itself becomes the anchor of the scene—not merely a practical object but a conduit for Leech's fascination with how light transforms surfaces and feelings.

Rather than painting a portrait in the traditional sense, Leech creates a mood, a fleeting instant of introspective leisure. The woman—widely believed to be his wife, Elizabeth—appears both present and remote, immersed in her own thoughts. The parasol's translucent fabric glows, casting a halo of filtered light across her face and dress, and with it, Leech offers a kind of visual sigh: a soft, meditative exhale captured in oil.

IMPRESSIONISM WITH AN IRISH ACCENT

Born in Dublin in 1881, William John Leech was one of Ireland's most refined (post) impressionist painters. His studies took him to Paris, where he absorbed the stylistic innovations of French Impressionism and Post-Impressionism. In *The Sunshade*, one can trace these influences: the loose brushwork, the emphasis on light over line, the compositional openness reminiscent of artists like Renoir and Vuillard.

However, Leech's work is not merely derivative. He infused the impressionist idiom with his own cultural lens—a mixture of Celtic restraint and continental exuberance. *The Sunshade* is not crowded with the bustle of urban life or ornate opulence; instead, it resonates with gentleness and quietude, hallmarks of Leech's distinctive voice.

A PERSONAL WORLD

Leech painted *The Sunshade* during a productive period spent in the coastal town of Concarneau, Brittany. It was here that he frequently depicted domestic scenes and luminous gardens, often using his wife and family as subjects. The intimacy of this setting and relationship translates into the canvas. It is both a universal depiction of summer idleness and a personal record of a loved one observed with tenderness.

The choice of a sunshade—a feminine accessory—also plays into subtle dynamics of privacy and gaze. Leech neither reveals nor obscures; instead, he invites us into a moment of gentle ambiguity. It's as if we've stumbled upon the scene from a respectful distance, allowed to look but not to intrude.

LEGACY IN STILLNESS

Although Leech never achieved the widespread fame of some of his contemporaries, *The Sunshade* stands as a testament to his artistry and vision. It now resides in the National Gallery of Ireland, quietly enthralling viewers more than a century later with its understated beauty.

In an age increasingly defined by noise and velocity, *The Sunshade* reminds us of the value of stillness. It asks us to pause, to consider how light can soften the edges of reality, and to rediscover the subtle pleasures that dwell in the everyday. Through Leech's brush, a simple afternoon becomes eternal.

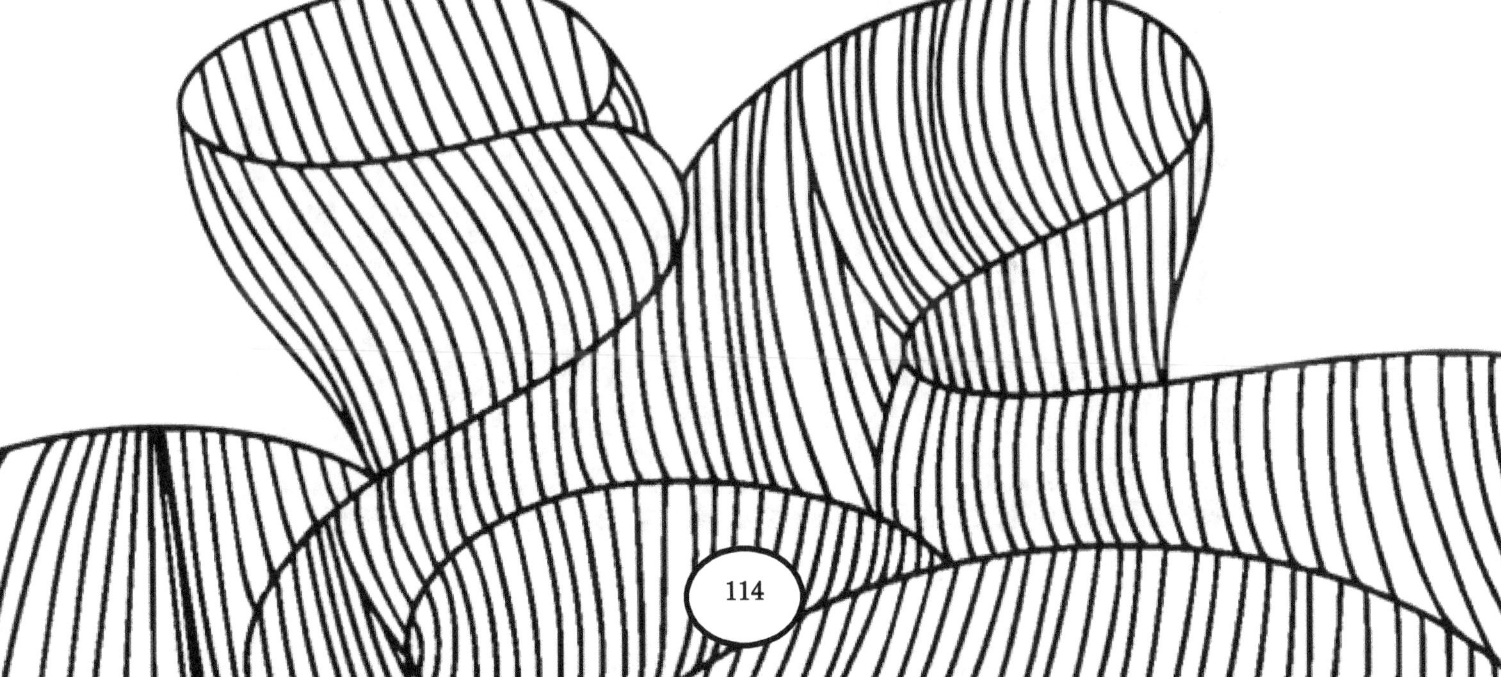

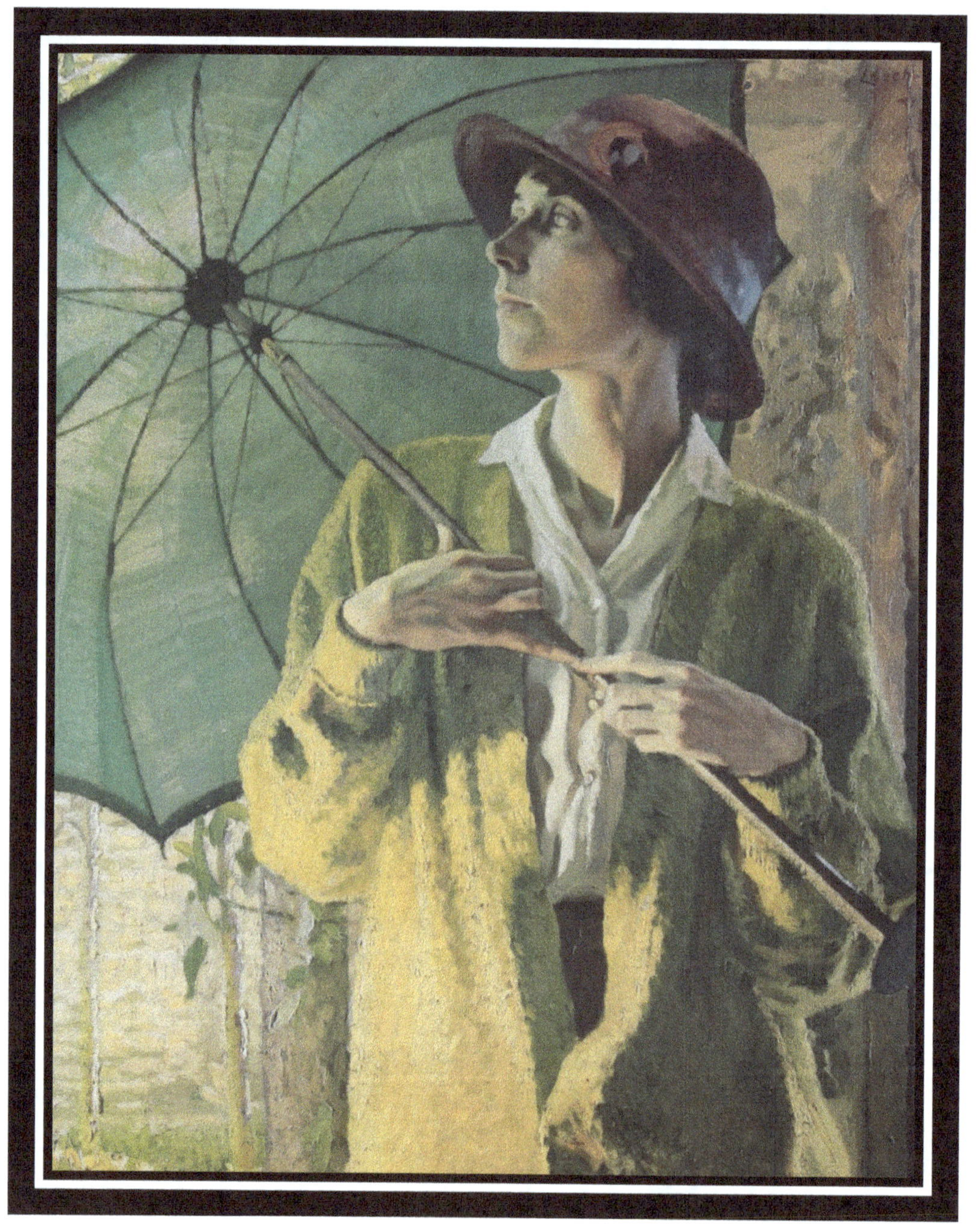

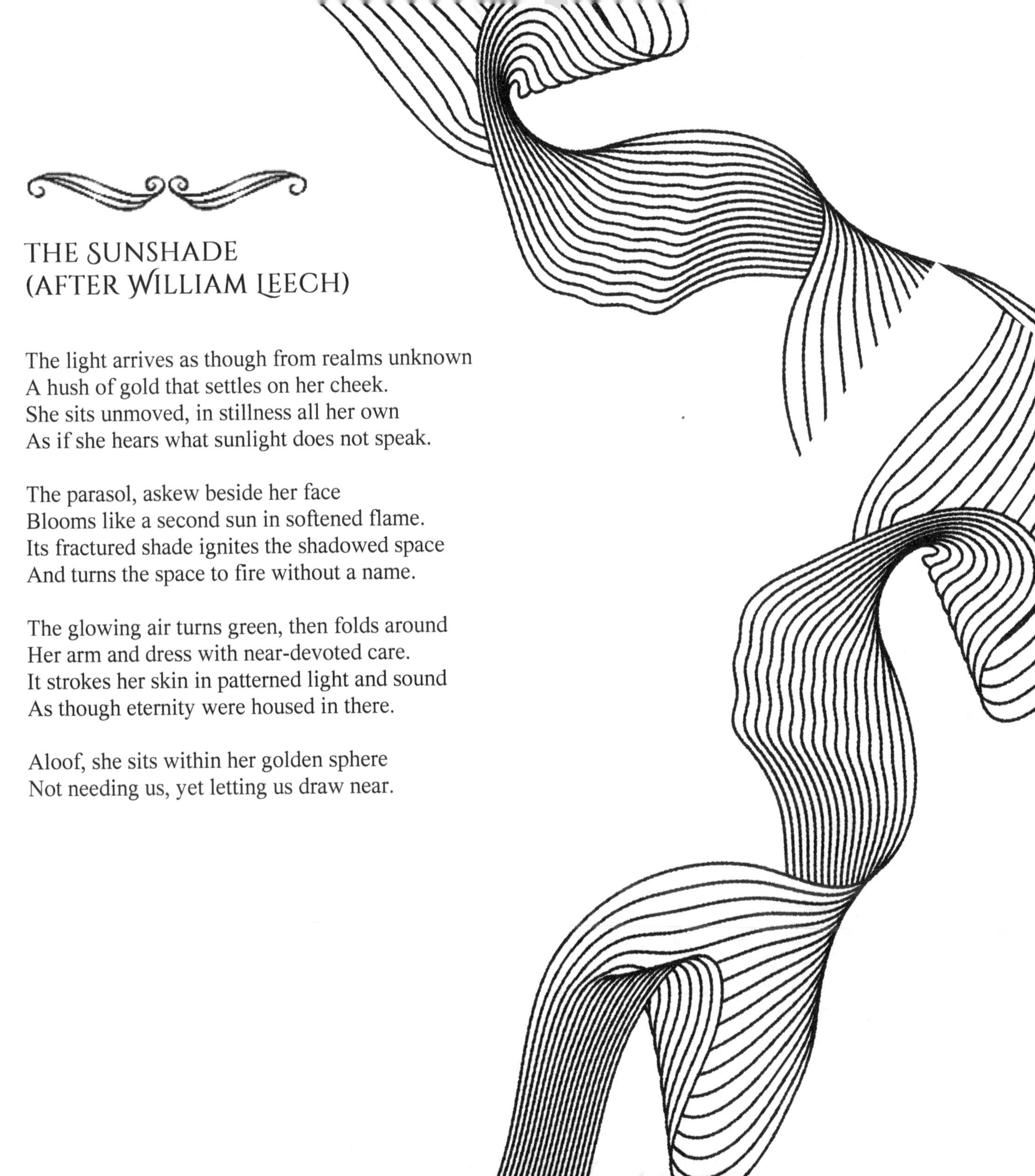

THE SUNSHADE
(AFTER WILLIAM LEECH)

The light arrives as though from realms unknown
A hush of gold that settles on her cheek.
She sits unmoved, in stillness all her own
As if she hears what sunlight does not speak.

The parasol, askew beside her face
Blooms like a second sun in softened flame.
Its fractured shade ignites the shadowed space
And turns the space to fire without a name.

The glowing air turns green, then folds around
Her arm and dress with near-devoted care.
It strokes her skin in patterned light and sound
As though eternity were housed in there.

Aloof, she sits within her golden sphere
Not needing us, yet letting us draw near.

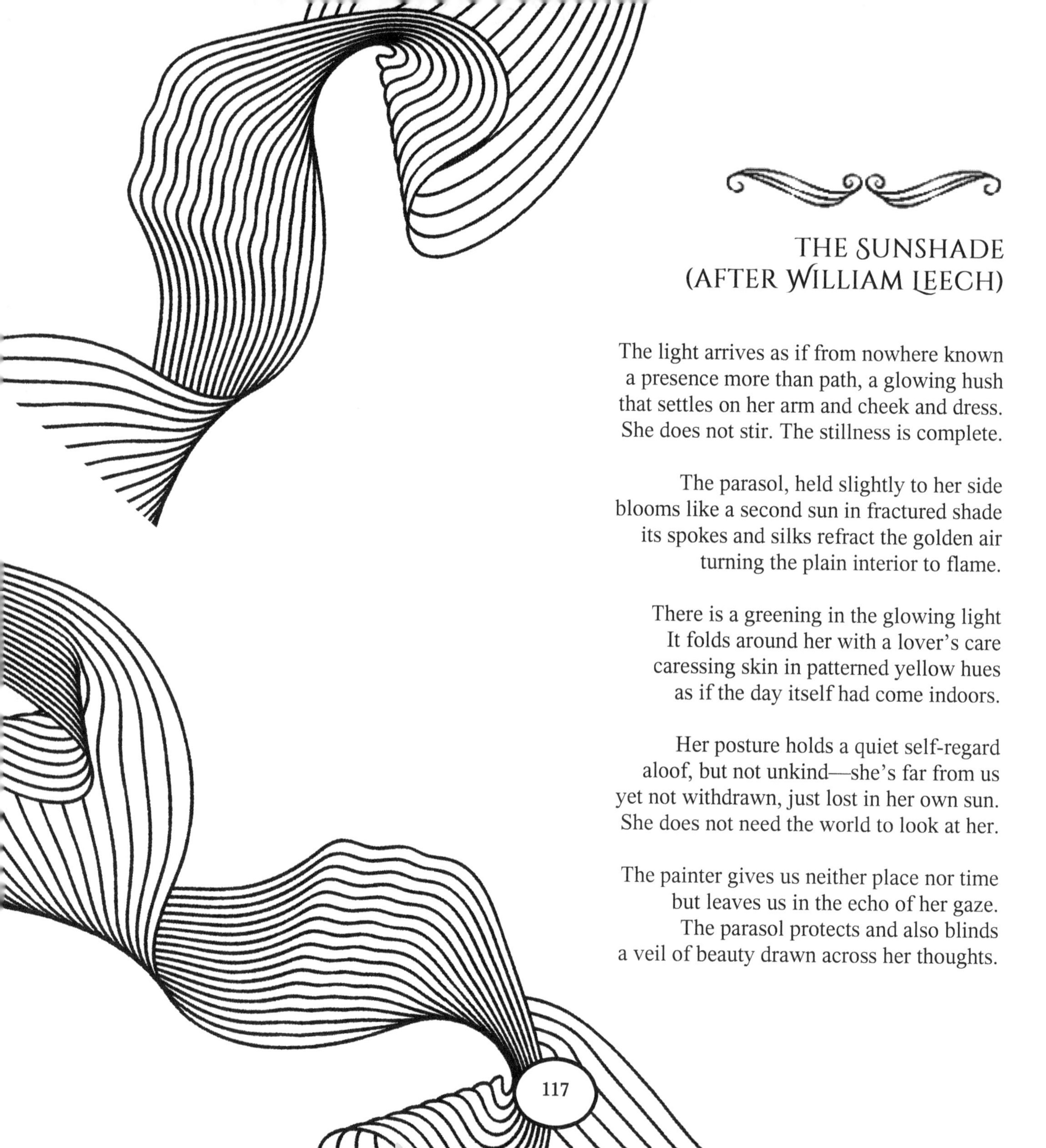

THE SUNSHADE
(AFTER WILLIAM LEECH)

The light arrives as if from nowhere known
a presence more than path, a glowing hush
that settles on her arm and cheek and dress.
She does not stir. The stillness is complete.

The parasol, held slightly to her side
blooms like a second sun in fractured shade
its spokes and silks refract the golden air
turning the plain interior to flame.

There is a greening in the glowing light
It folds around her with a lover's care
caressing skin in patterned yellow hues
as if the day itself had come indoors.

Her posture holds a quiet self-regard
aloof, but not unkind—she's far from us
yet not withdrawn, just lost in her own sun.
She does not need the world to look at her.

The painter gives us neither place nor time
but leaves us in the echo of her gaze.
The parasol protects and also blinds
a veil of beauty drawn across her thoughts.

TEARS IN COLOUR

UNPACKING THE EMOTIONAL LANDSCAPE OF PICASSO'S THE WEEPING WOMAN

Pablo Picasso's *The Weeping Woman* (1937) is not merely a portrait; it is a scream preserved in paint. Crafted during one of the darkest chapters of 20th-century history, this artwork transcends the realm of personal grief and plunges into the collective anguish of a nation torn apart by civil war. Its jagged geometry, shrill palette, and distorted anatomy force the viewer into an uneasy intimacy with sorrow.

A FRAGMENT FROM *GUERNICA'S* ECHO

To understand *The Weeping Woman*, one must first stand in the long shadow of *Guernica*. That massive anti-war mural, created in response to the brutal bombing of the Basque town during the Spanish Civil War, lays bare the trauma of violence. Within *Guernica*, a small figure—an anguished woman clutching her dead child—emerges as the emotional epicentre. Picasso would return to this figure again and again, exploring her suffering in standalone works, culminating in *The Weeping Woman*.

This particular painting, housed today in the Tate Modern in London, is not a single cry—it is the amplification of a thousand. The woman's face is fractured, as if splintered by grief itself. Her eyes pour stylized tears that resemble sharp shards of glass. Her handkerchief seems frozen in a desperate, futile gesture of control. In Picasso's vision, pain is not passive—it erupts, convulses, and deforms.

DORA MAAR – MUSE, MIRROR, AND MORE

The physical model for *The Weeping Woman* was Dora Maar, Picasso's lover and muse. Maar was an accomplished artist and intellectual in her own right, whose relationship with Picasso was both creatively fertile and emotionally turbulent. Picasso once described her as the embodiment of grief, claiming, "For me, she's the weeping woman."

However, reducing the portrait to a mere depiction of Maar would be to miss the deeper metaphor. The woman in this painting is not just Dora. She is Spain. She is every mother, wife, or daughter whose life was splintered by war. In that sense, she becomes a universal symbol of mourning.

COLOUR AS EMOTION, NOT DECORATION

One of the most disarming elements of *The Weeping Woman* is its use of colour. Unlike conventional depictions of sorrow cloaked in muted blues or greys, Picasso uses fiery oranges, acidic yellows, and electric greens. These are not calming tones—they are aggressive, chaotic, acidic. They assault the senses, refusing to let the viewer grieve quietly.

In Cubist fashion, Picasso fractures and reassembles form to suggest multiplicity of perspective. But here, the formal experimentation carries emotional weight. Her face, torn into conflicting planes, mirrors the psychological fragmentation of trauma. The dislocation is not just visual—it is existential.

AN IMAGE THAT REFUSES TO FADE

Over the decades, *The Weeping Woman* has become one of Picasso's most reproduced and analysed images. Yet it retains a rawness that resists sterilisation. Its power lies in its refusal to resolve or soothe. It does not offer catharsis—it offers confrontation.

Even today, in a world still punctuated by conflict and forced displacement, *The Weeping Woman* remains profoundly relevant. Her tears may be painted, but their resonance is real. She reminds us that art can be more than a reflection—it can be a cry, a witness, a warning.

In the canon of Picasso's work, *The Weeping Woman* is not the grandest nor the most technically complex. But it may be the most human. In her fractured face, we recognise our own moments of breaking. And in her ceaseless weeping, we find a call not only to feel—but to remember.

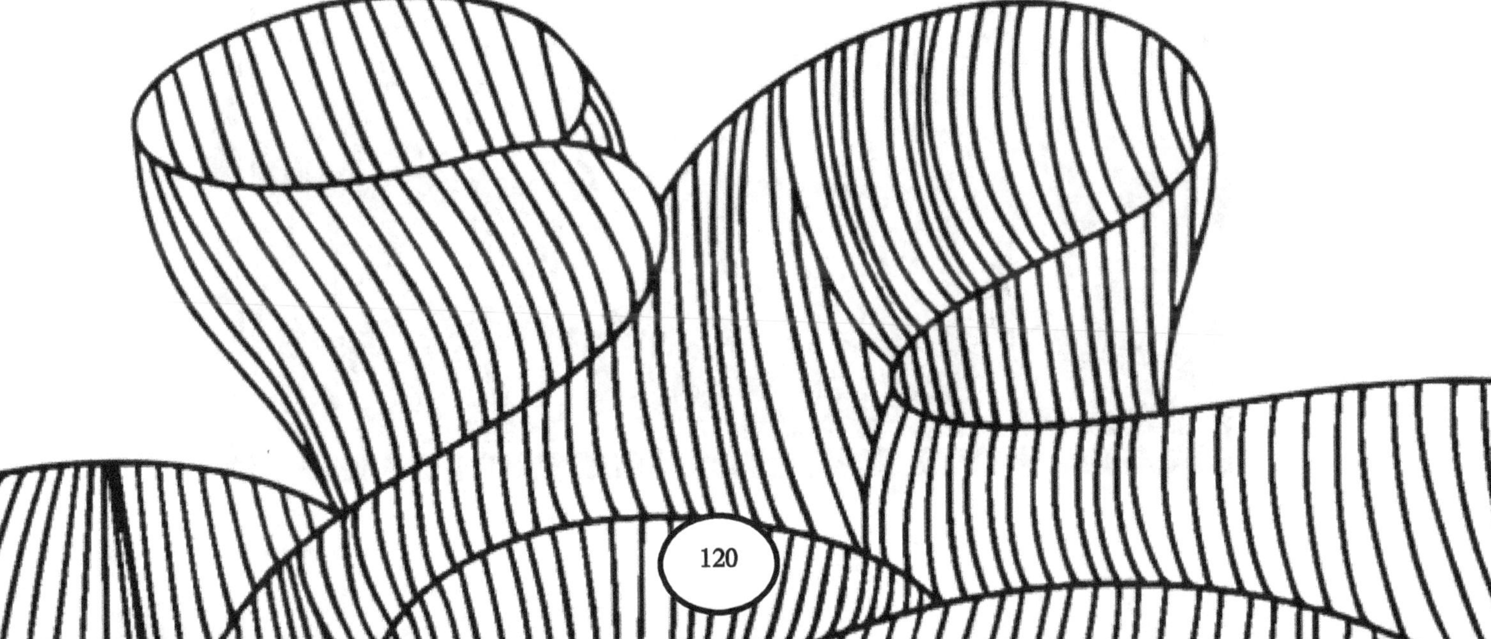

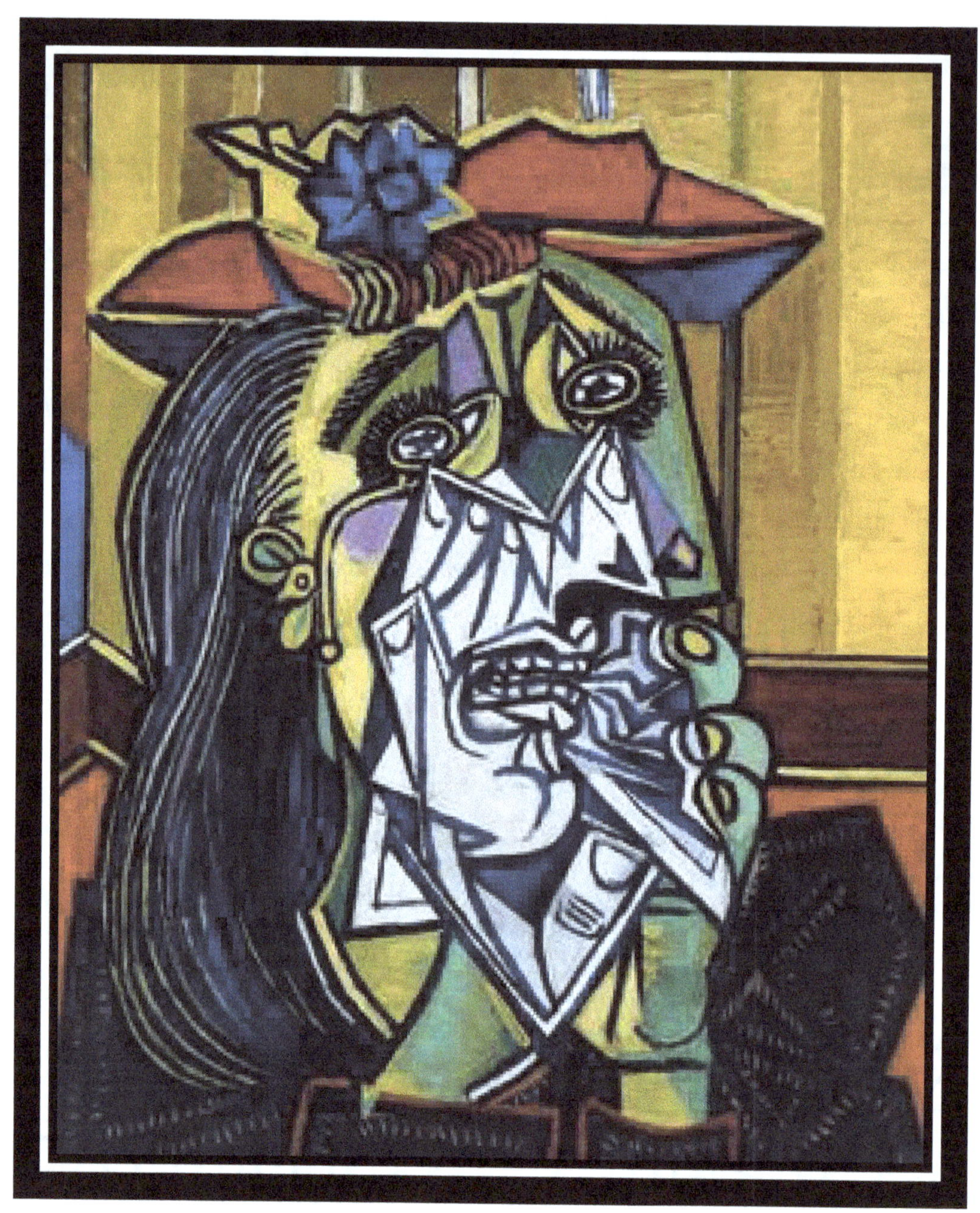

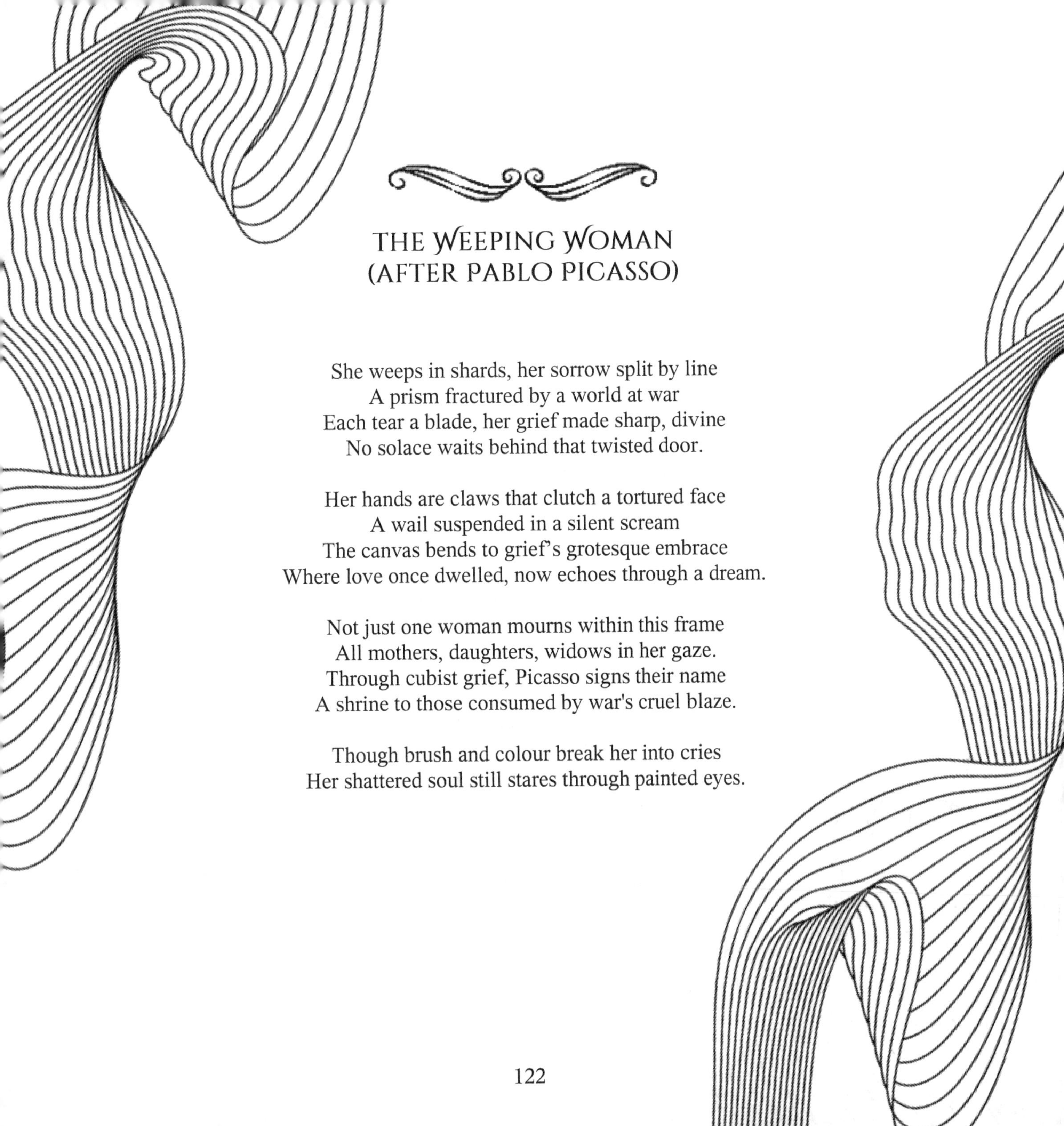

THE WEEPING WOMAN
(AFTER PABLO PICASSO)

She weeps in shards, her sorrow split by line
A prism fractured by a world at war
Each tear a blade, her grief made sharp, divine
No solace waits behind that twisted door.

Her hands are claws that clutch a tortured face
A wail suspended in a silent scream
The canvas bends to grief's grotesque embrace
Where love once dwelled, now echoes through a dream.

Not just one woman mourns within this frame
All mothers, daughters, widows in her gaze.
Through cubist grief, Picasso signs their name
A shrine to those consumed by war's cruel blaze.

Though brush and colour break her into cries
Her shattered soul still stares through painted eyes.

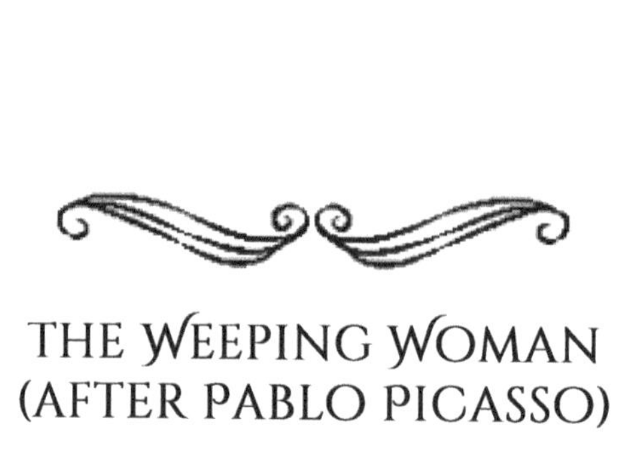

THE WEEPING WOMAN
(AFTER PABLO PICASSO)

She sits in silence, yet the silence screams
a fractured face, all angles, sharp with grief.
No comfort lies within her painted hands
that twist and clutch as if to hold back time.

Her mouth, a cage, distorts a sob mid-birth
caught in the act of mourning something vast
not just a child, a lover, or a dream
but all that war can strip from flesh and soul.

Each line is jagged, violence in form
a chaos calcified by palette knife.
The tears are green, like bile or acid rain
and soak the canvas with a nameless ache.

This woman, though alone, is not herself
she is a mirror cracked by history,
her sorrow stitched from Spain's unravelling.
Picasso does not offer her release
but binds her pain in oil and bitter light.

She weeps, and in her weeping we remain
forever staring back into her loss.

Frida Kahlo's Self-Portrait with Thorn Necklace and Hummingbird

A Vivid Testament of Pain and Power

Frida Kahlo's 1940 painting *Autorretrato con Collar de Espinas y Colibrí* (*Self-Portrait with Thorn Necklace and Hummingbird*) is far more than a self-representation—it is a psychological map, a symbolic declaration of resilience, and a meditation on the fusion of suffering and beauty. This artwork captures the complex layers of Kahlo's identity: her physical torment, emotional solitude, cultural heritage, and indomitable will.

At first glance, the painting presents a stoic, symmetrical Kahlo, her expression calm yet distant. Her signature unibrow and moustache are rendered unapologetically, an intentional affirmation of self that resists conventional beauty norms. Yet beneath the surface of stillness, a cacophony of visual symbols pulses with quiet intensity.

THE THORN NECKLACE – SACRED SUFFERING

Around Kahlo's neck is a thorn necklace, tightly wound and digging into her skin, drawing delicate rivulets of blood. This self-inflicted crown of suffering immediately evokes Christian iconography, particularly that of Christ's crown of thorns. Kahlo transforms martyrdom into personal narrative—her necklace is both shield and shackle. It references her lifelong battle with pain, particularly following a traumatic bus accident in her youth, but also speaks to the broader suffering of being a woman, an artist, and a Mexican mestiza navigating a colonised, patriarchal world.

The choice of thorns is deliberate: they are natural yet violent, beautiful yet cruel. Kahlo doesn't shy away from discomfort—instead, she wears it openly, making the invisible visible.

THE HUMMINGBIRD – FLIGHT, LOVE, AND PARADOX

Dangling lifelessly from the necklace is a black hummingbird, a bird traditionally associated with vitality, joy, and freedom. In Mexican folklore, hummingbirds can be seen as messengers between the living and the dead, or as tokens of good luck in love. Here, however, the bird is limp, almost crucified, its wings outstretched in a subtle echo of the cross.

This dead hummingbird is not a symbol of hope, but of lost love and broken spirit—possibly referencing her tumultuous relationship with Diego Rivera or the broader loss of romantic idealism. Yet even in its death, the bird retains a talismanic presence, challenging the viewer to consider how beauty and despair so often coexist.

JUNGLE AS PSYCHE: THE SURREAL LANDSCAPE

Behind Kahlo, the verdant backdrop teems with thick leaves and an almost suffocating presence of flora. This dense jungle is not paradise—it feels claustrophobic, encroaching, as though her inner world is overgrown with tangled emotions. From the foliage emerge two companions: a black cat and a monkey.

The black cat, perched ominously on her left shoulder, is a classical symbol of bad luck and witchcraft. Its alert, menacing stare seems to guard her or perhaps haunt her, a shadow of fate or death. In contrast, the monkey on her right, a gift from Rivera, appears almost tender. Yet it tugs at the thorn necklace, tightening it further—a gentle figure causing harm. Kahlo again invites paradox: comfort and pain are often entwined.

EMBLEM OF THE PERSONAL AS POLITICAL

What makes *Self-Portrait with Thorn Necklace and Hummingbird* so powerful is its unapologetic embrace of the personal as a form of protest. Kahlo does not idealise herself—she mythologises her lived reality. Her unflinching self-portrait becomes a revolutionary act, defying both Western standards of beauty and sanitised depictions of femininity.

The painting is not merely autobiographical; it is metaphysical. It collapses time, culture, and identity into a singular frame, inviting the viewer to confront not just Kahlo's pain, but their own. Each symbol—whether the thorn, the hummingbird, or the jungle—acts as a mirror, reflecting the fractured yet beautiful landscapes of human experience.

AN ICON BEYOND THE CANVAS

In *Self-Portrait with Thorn Necklace and Hummingbird*, Frida Kahlo cements her legacy not as a painter of suffering, but as a master of emotional alchemy. She transforms anguish into visual poetry, silence into colour, and passivity into power. This painting is not a cry—it is a quiet, steady gaze that pierces through time, challenging us to look back with equal honesty and courage.

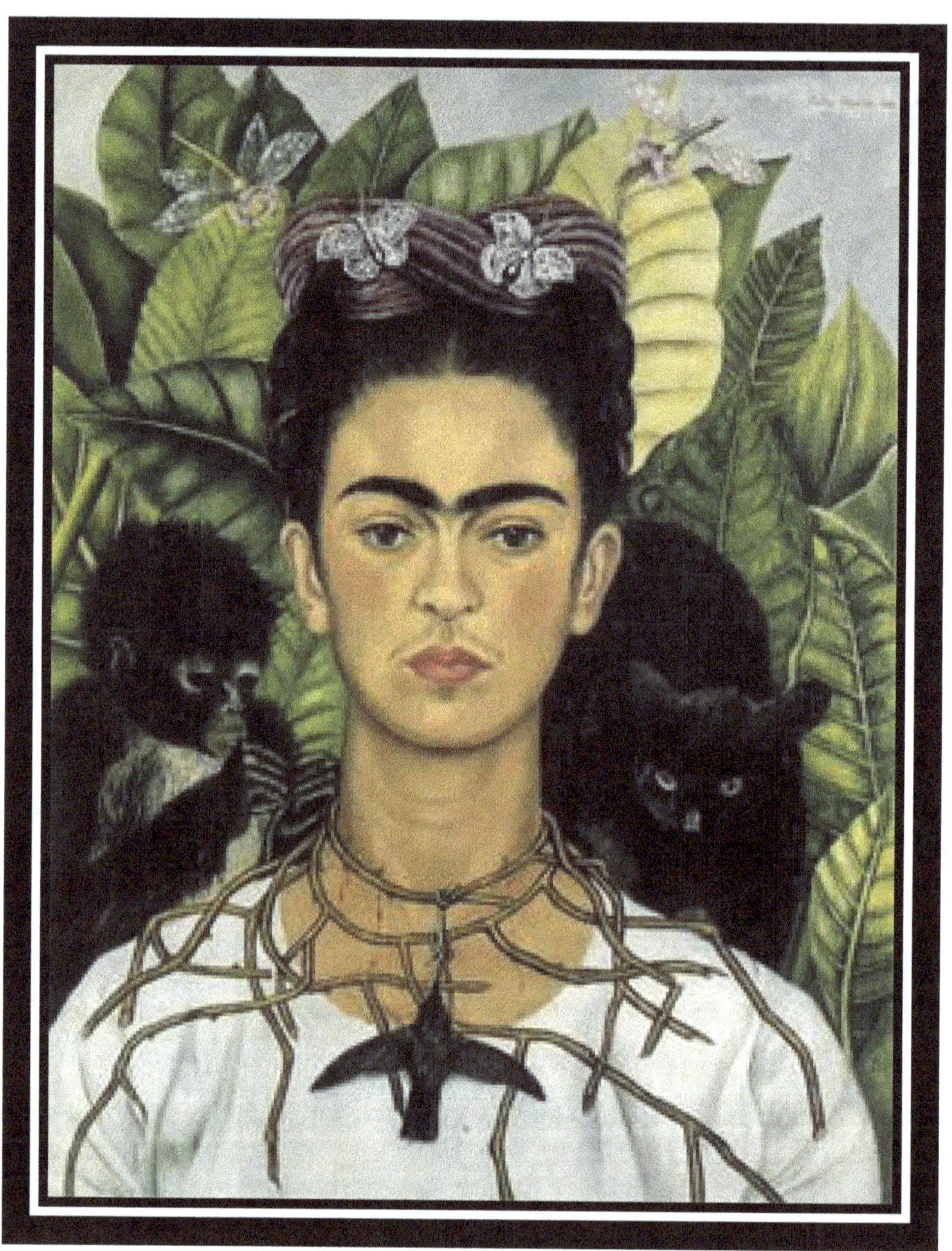

SELF-PORTRAIT WITH THORN NECKLACE AND HUMMINGBIRD
(AFTER FRIDA KAHLO)

You meet me with a gaze that does not plead—
Unbowed, though thorns have kissed your throat to red.
The jungle crowds, but you command its seed
Even the hummingbird hangs, fierce instead.

What are you queen of, Frida? Pain, or fire?
A martyr in the dress of flesh and root?
The monkey's hand—curious, not entire—
Holds still, as if it knows you are the fruit.

You wear your suffering like saints wear light
Not asking mercy, only to be seen.
The cat behind you sharpens out of sight
A shadow coiled in leaves, composed and lean.

Your silence speaks: *I am not what I seem.*
This isn't portrait—it's a waking dream.

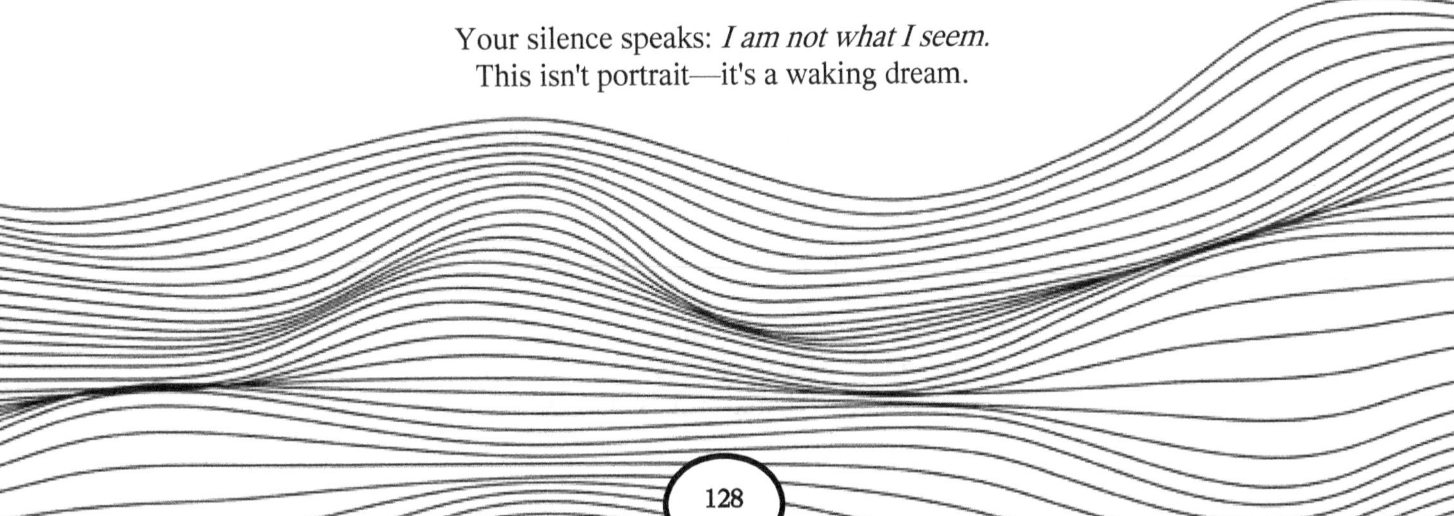

STILLNESS THAT REFUSES TO BREAK
(AFTER FRIDA KAHLO)

What does it mean to suffer into form?
To shape the self with thorns instead of tools—
to frame a face not as the world would see
but as the self observes its own undoing?

Her eyes do not accuse. They simply are.
A fact. A presence forged beyond appeal.
She does not ask to be interpreted.
She is the meaning, and the one who makes.

The thorns are time—each barb a counted cost.
Pain made visible, arranged, adorned, endured.
She does not turn away. To turn would lie.
To flinch would grant the world the final word.

The bird beneath her throat suspends belief.
It does not fly, yet pulses with not-flight.
A paradox: the ache for motion held
by will alone—resistance without rage.
Is this not freedom, too? To not escape
but hold one's suffering so still, it sings?

Behind her, nature lurks in borrowed forms—
the monkey like a second self, detached
untouched but tethered still by gaze and thorn.

The cat, pure instinct dressed in watching skin
reminds the soul that beauty is not kind.

And yet she does not yield to either force.
She stands between the animal and god
between the wound and what the wound reveals.

This is not just a portrait. It's a claim
I am the one who sees, and still is seen.
I am the thorn, the gaze, the stillest flame.

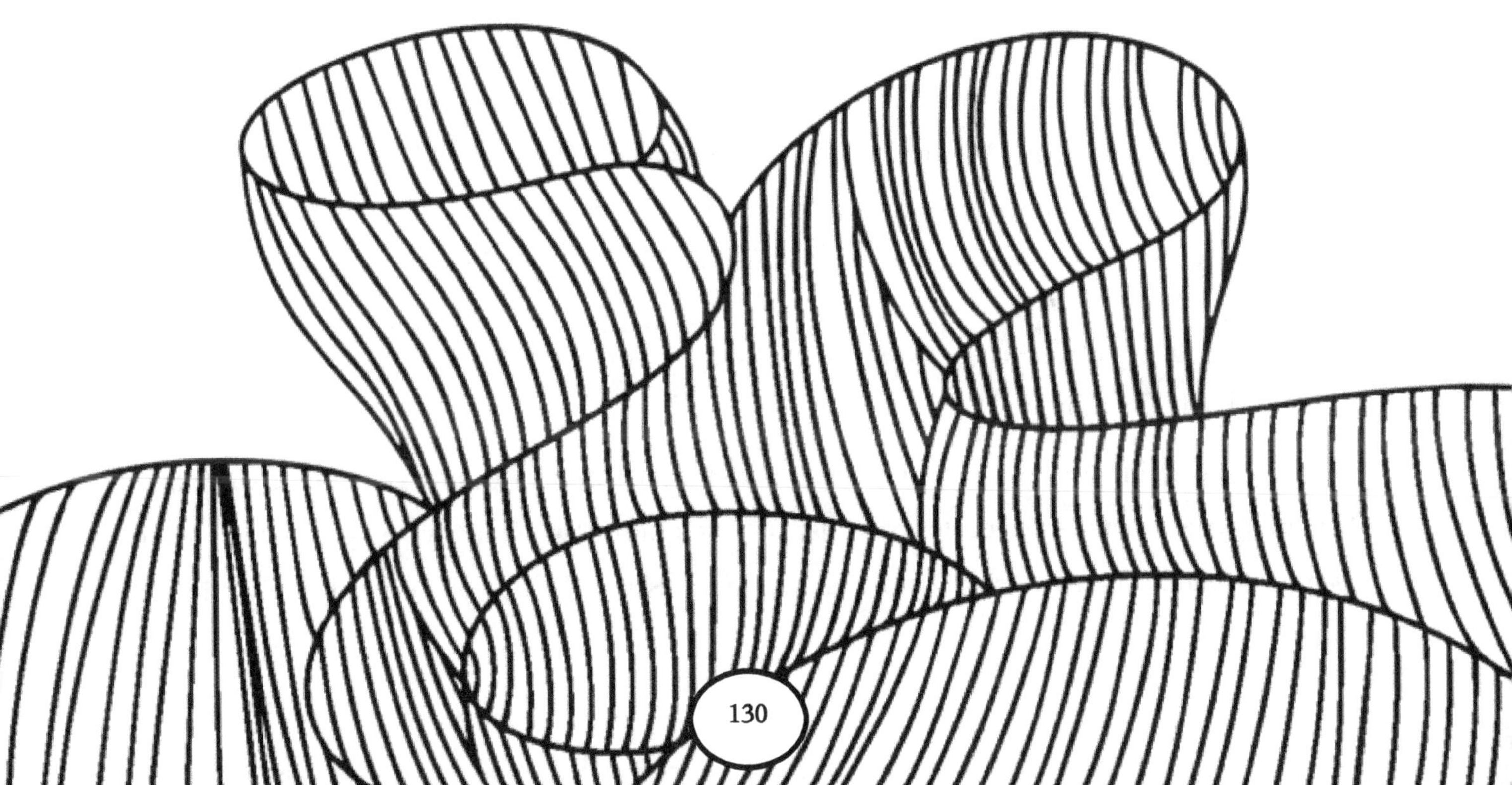

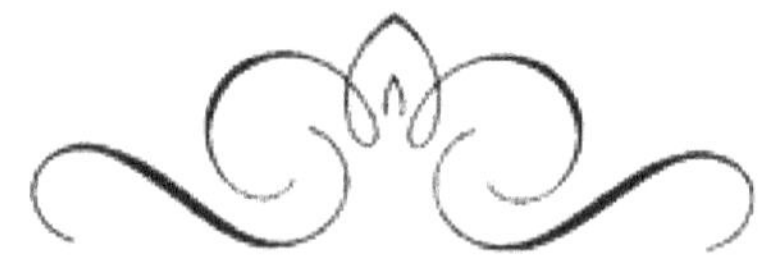

Spiritual Drama and Baroque Innovation

THE CONVERSION OF SAINT PAUL ON THE ROAD TO DAMASCUS BY CARAVAGGIO

Painted by Michelangelo Merisi da Caravaggio in 1601 *The Conversion of Saint Paul on the Road to Damascus*, is one of the most powerful visual expressions of spiritual transformation in Western art. Commissioned as part of a pair for the Cerasi Chapel in the Church of Santa Maria del Popolo in Rome, the painting exemplifies Caravaggio's revolutionary approach to religious subject matter and his hallmark use of dramatic realism and chiaroscuro.

SUBJECT AND CONTEXT

The painting depicts a pivotal moment from the Acts of the Apostles (Acts 9:3-6), in which Saul of Tarsus—zealous persecutor of Christians—is struck down by a divine light on the road to Damascus and hears the voice of Christ asking, "Saul, Saul, why do you persecute me?" Blinded and humbled, Saul experiences a profound spiritual awakening, eventually becoming Paul, the apostle to the Gentiles.

Caravaggio's version breaks from tradition in both composition and emotion. Rather than a panoramic biblical scene filled with heavenly figures, the viewer is confronted with an intimate, tightly cropped moment of vulnerability. Paul lies on the ground, arms stretched open, in a posture that evokes both surrender and spiritual ecstasy. A horse looms above him, held back by a groom, both seemingly unaware of the extraordinary vision Paul is experiencing.

COMPOSITION AND STYLE

Caravaggio's masterful use of tenebrism—the stark contrast of light and dark—places Paul's conversion in a supernatural yet believable world. The divine light that seizes Paul is not symbolised by cherubs or radiant skies, but through a shaft of illumination that pierces the darkness, making Paul's figure glow with emotional intensity. The ground-level perspective draws the viewer into the drama, collapsing the distance between sacred history and contemporary reality.

The horse, occupying nearly half the canvas, has been the subject of much scholarly debate. Some critics suggest that its dominant presence symbolises Paul's former pride and power, which has now been overthrown. Others argue that its placid demeanour reflects the natural world's indifference to divine revelation—underscoring the intensely personal nature of Paul's transformation.

INTERPRETATION AND IMPACT

Caravaggio's interpretation of the scene is radical. By stripping away overt religious iconography, he focuses instead on the *humanity* of conversion. Paul is not a distant saint but a man in crisis, caught in a moment of overwhelming grace. His closed eyes suggest that the revelation is internal; the viewer sees what Paul cannot. This internalisation of the divine marks a departure from the Renaissance ideal of glorified saints and emphasises the emotional realism that came to define Baroque art.

The work also reflects the Counter-Reformation ideals promoted by the Catholic Church. In response to Protestant iconoclasm, the Church sought emotionally resonant and didactic images to inspire piety and awe. Caravaggio delivered exactly that—religious drama rooted in real, physical bodies and genuine emotional response.

LEGACY

The Conversion of Saint Paul on the Road to Damascus remains one of Caravaggio's most iconic works, influencing countless artists after him, including Rembrandt, Rubens, and later Romantic painters. Its psychological depth and naturalistic portrayal of the sacred contributed to a new understanding of how the divine could be rendered in art—not as remote and stylised, but as imminent and deeply human.

Through this painting, Caravaggio transformed a moment of biblical conversion into a timeless meditation on humility, faith, and the mystery of divine intervention.

A STORY OF TRANSFORMATION

Caravaggio's *Conversion of Saint Paul* is not just a religious painting; it is a deeply human story of transformation, captured with unprecedented immediacy and empathy. More than four centuries after it was painted, it still challenges viewers to reflect on the nature of revelation, the limits of perception, and the possibility of redemption.

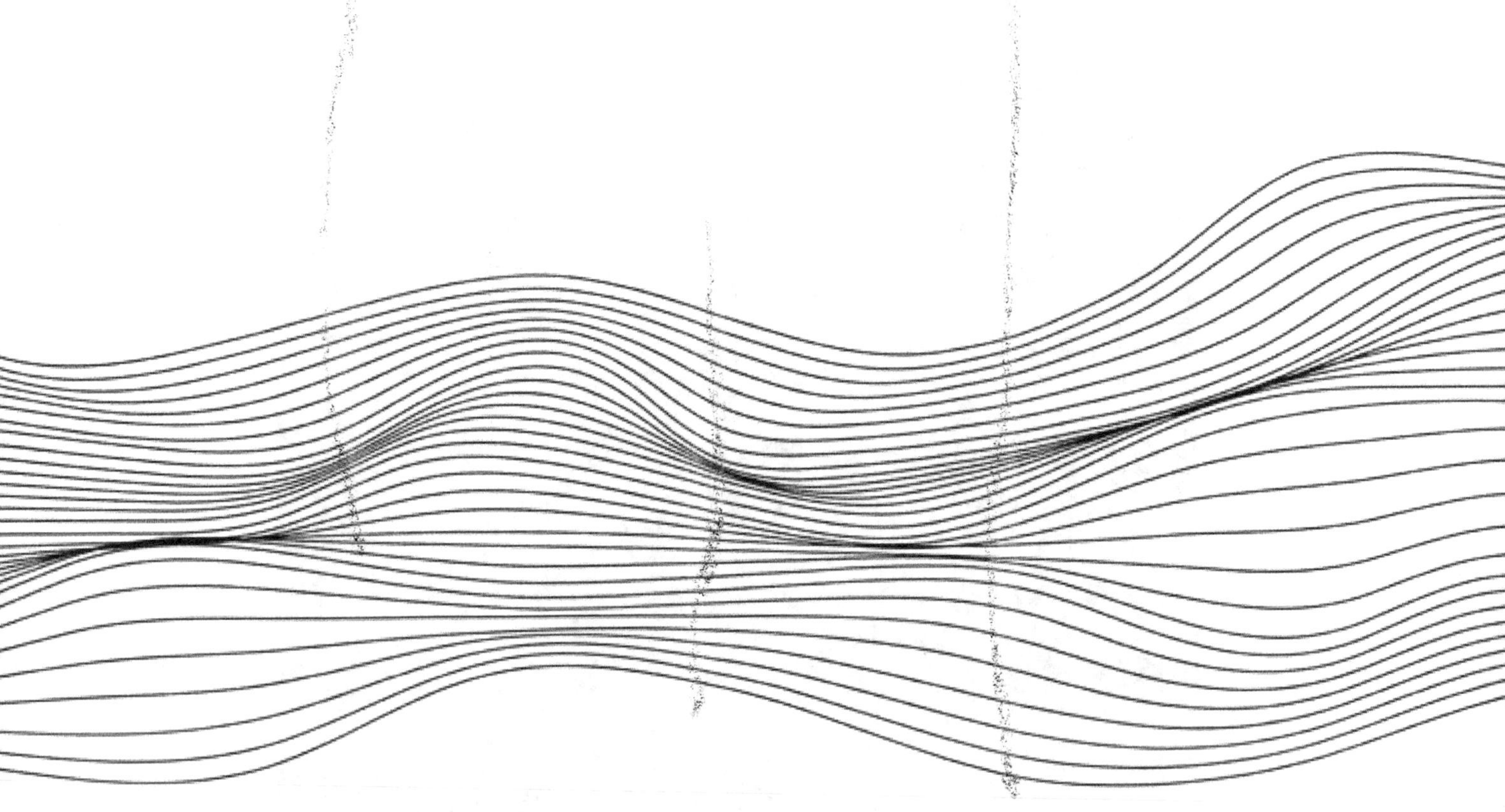

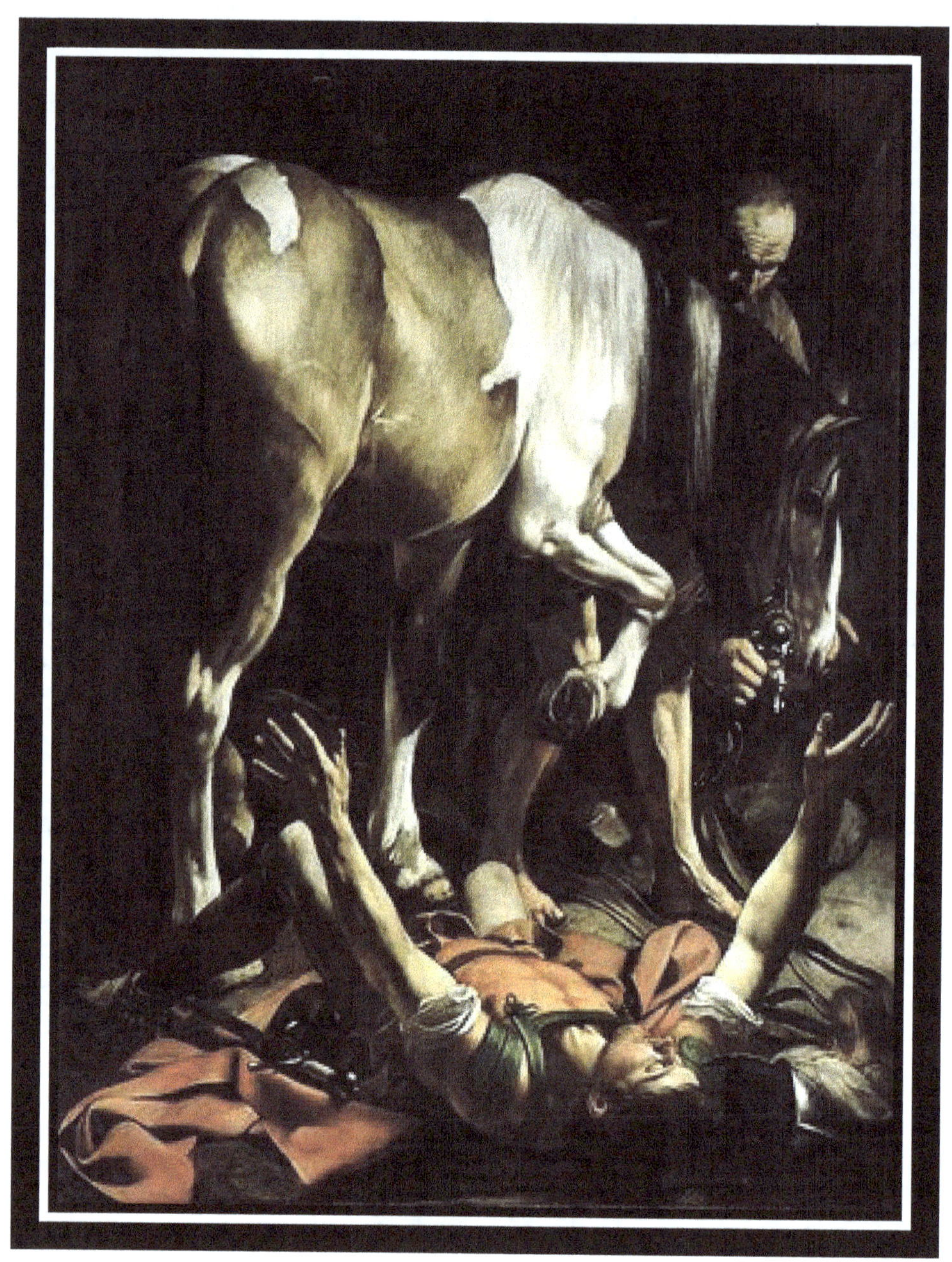

THE LIGHT THAT THREW HIM LOW
(AFTER CARAVAGGIO)

He falls, not from the horse but from his pride
Arms flung to catch a grace he cannot see—
The dazzled soldier cast in shadow wide
While heaven strikes with fierce humility.
The beast stands calm, its eyes a mute rebuke
As Paul lies blind beneath the sudden flame
No thunder speaks, no angels veil or look—
Just light, and silence, and a whispered name.

Caravaggio knew this fall from height
That blinding truth is born from darkest ground
And saints are not made clean by gentle light
But by a voice that breaks, then turns them round.
So lies the man, undone in violent peace—
A soul arrested for its slow release.

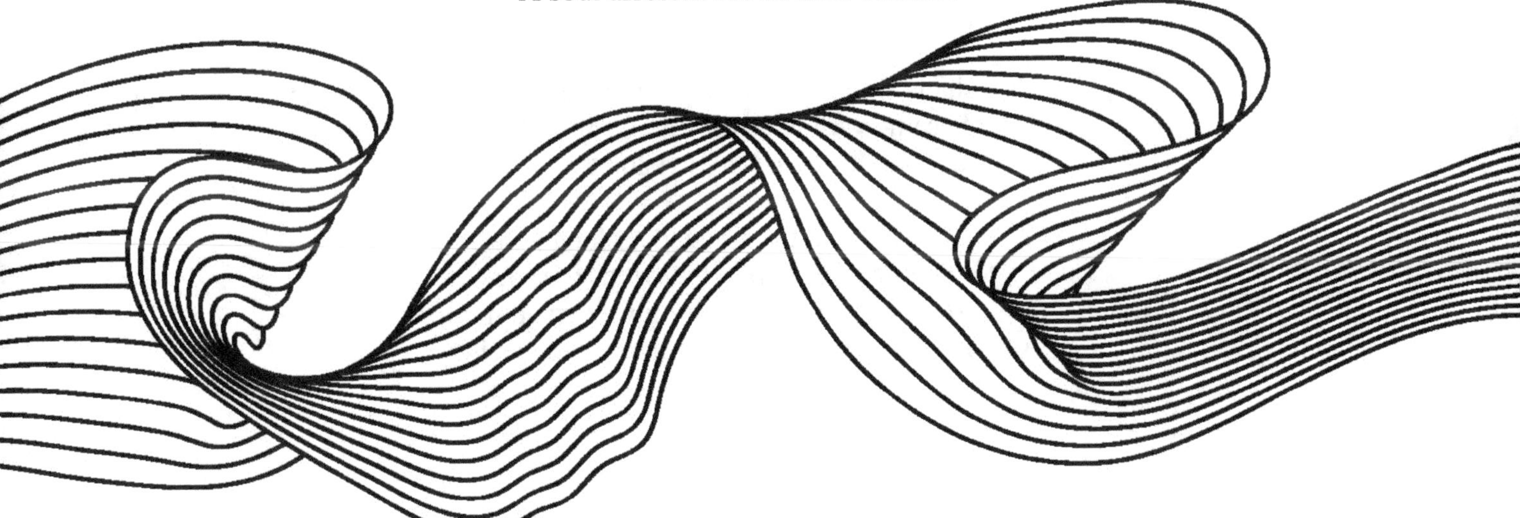

THE CONVERSION OF SAINT PAUL ON THE ROAD TO DAMASCUS
(AFTER CARAVAGGIO)

A flash of light descends upon the road
More fierce than day, yet silent in its weight.
The horse rears back, its eyes gone wide with flame
While Saul lies prone, his arms flung toward the void.

The darkness gathers round the painter's frame—
Not void, but velvet soaked in sacred dread.
A servant holds the reins with quiet hands
Unmoved by fire that cleaves the mortal air.

What voice does Saul now hear behind closed eyes?
It splits his name in twain – then binds it whole.
The dust clings tight to his skin like a shroud
And heaven speaks to earth from throne or cloud.

The fingers stretch, as if to touch the light
Or shield the self from knowledge undesired.
He came with wrath to blind a city's kin
And found his own fierce vision torn away.

No angels flood the sky with golden wings
No choir ascends upon the winds of grace.
Just hooves and cloth and shadows carved in oil
And one man's soul laid bare beneath the weight.

Painter, master of chiaroscuro
You show the fall as first step toward the rise.
The path to God lies not in conquest won
But in the stillness where all strength gives way.

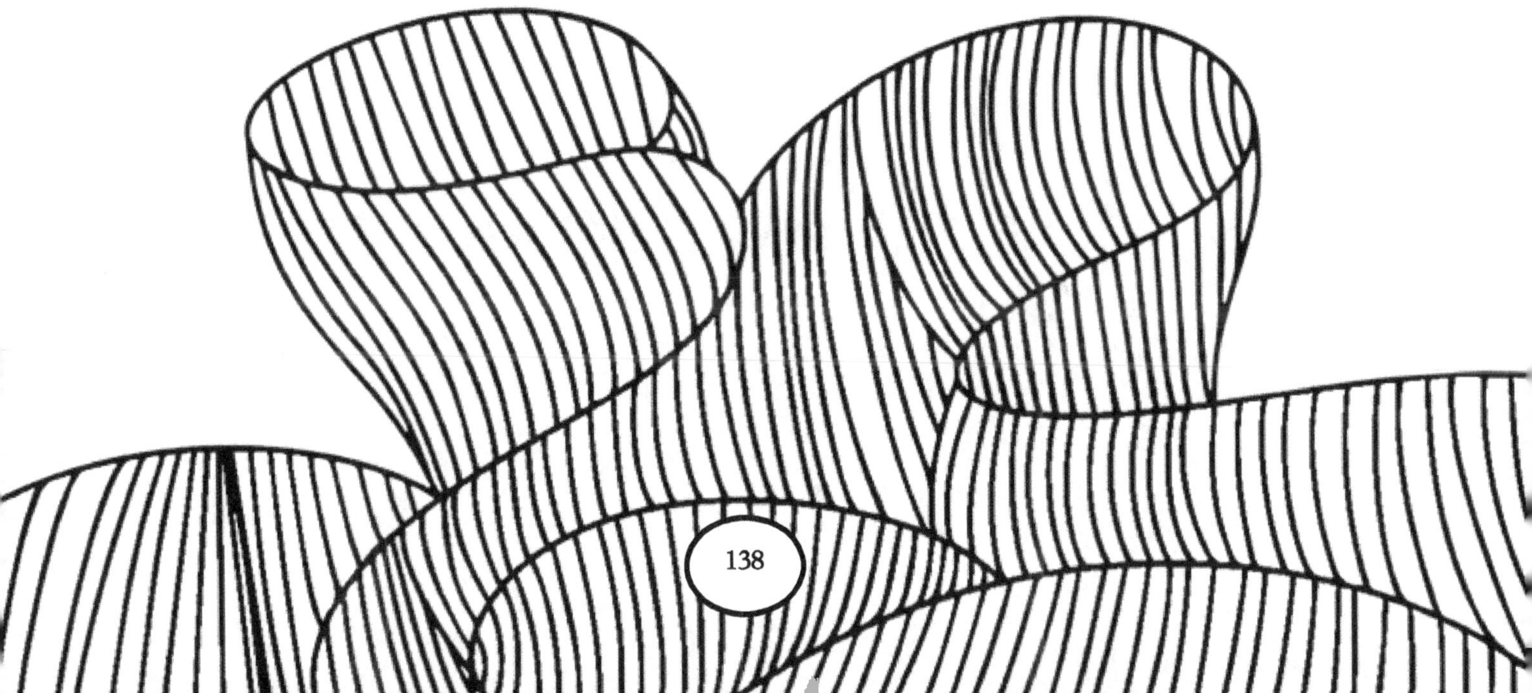